INDOOR PLAY

Written by Ellen Moshein

Illustrated by Kelly McMahon

Photography by Anthony Nex

McGraw-Hill
Children's Publishing
A Division of The *McGraw·Hill* Companies

Published by Frank Schaffer Publications
An imprint of McGraw-Hill Children's Publishing
Copyright © 1997 McGraw-Hill Children's Publishing

Send all inquiries to:
McGraw-Hill Children's Publishing
3195 Wilson Drive NW
Grand Rapids, Michigan 49544

Indoor Play
ISBN: 0-7647-0275-0

Table of Contents

INTRODUCTION

This book is intended for use as a resource for teaching physical education. The games and activities are simple to learn, simple to teach, and lots of challenging fun for the students! This book contains ideas for individual and cooperative games as well as tips on classroom management. Included in the games are several that require very little equipment but which encourage participation by every student. There is even an entire chapter devoted to activities using a classic and well-loved playground tool—the parachute. These parachute activities work very well in a gymnasium or multipurpose room. Suggestions for other noncompetitive indoor activities appear throughout the book. Finally, this book provides several award certificates to help celebrate the students' participation and success!

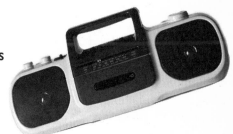

Any instructional leader can use the activities described in this book to help promote physical fitness in children. In doing so, a teacher can provide students with opportunities not only to succeed in physical education, but also to develop a lifelong commitment to the health benefits and pleasure of physical activity!

Physical education can be a useful interdisciplinary tool because it can provide an important boost to academics. Many of the skills which students learn during physical education activities directly correlate with skills they need for success in the classroom. Specifically, students learn to cooperate and communicate with each other as they participate in P.E. activities. They can develop a strong sense of camaraderie and team spirit during physical education. This, in turn, will help them rally together as a classroom. Further, these activities can help students strengthen their communication skills. As individuals working as a cooperative unit toward a common goal— as is done in a team sport—students necessarily sharpen their communication skills. Students learn how to lead, to take directions, to listen, and to encourage one another. These are skills that transfer directly into the classroom and into the larger community.

Students should experience fitness opportunities every day, regardless of the weather. On days when the weather keeps everyone indoors, fitness activities offer a fun, organized outlet for the extra energy students build up while staying inside for extended periods of time. Keeping the students active on bad weather days will get them moving, motivated, and ready for later, more academic learning.

Using indoor activities even in fair weather is a good way to keep any physical education program from becoming repetitive. So, during fair or inclement weather, indoor activities give the students alternatives for building health habits, showing the students that they can become physically fit both outdoors and indoors.

FS-32602 Indoor Play © Frank Schaffer Publications

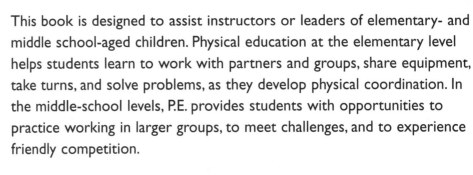

This book is designed to assist instructors or leaders of elementary- and middle school-aged children. Physical education at the elementary level helps students learn to work with partners and groups, share equipment, take turns, and solve problems, as they develop physical coordination. In the middle-school levels, P.E. provides students with opportunities to practice working in larger groups, to meet challenges, and to experience friendly competition.

The physical and social skill levels required for the activities and games in this book vary. Most of the activities and games are appropriate for different skill levels. It is very important that teachers keep in mind the physical and social capabilities of their particular students as they select activities for use in their programs. The level of difficulty is noted at the top of each activity so that the teacher can easily identify the most appropriate activities for his or her class.

The lowest level of difficulty is **simple**. Activities that are labeled as simple require a minimum level of physical skills. These games also require only a minimum amount of equipment and set-up time, and have a simple set of rules. Simple activities are ideal for primary students.

The next level of difficulty is **moderate**. Activities that are labeled as moderate require an intermediate level of physical coordination and skills. These activities likewise require a moderate amount of equipment and set-up time, and have a more complicated system of rules. These games require that students are capable of understanding multiple sets of instructions and can work cooperatively in small groups.

The highest level of difficulty is **challenging**. Activities that are labeled as challenging involve the need for high-level physical coordination, stamina, and manipulation skills. These activities often require more equipment and set-up time, and can have a complicated set of rules.

By choosing activities that are appropriate to the students' capability levels, teachers can ensure that the students will be able to achieve success during their physical education experiences. Once students enjoy success in their physical activities, success in other classroom activities is not far behind!

FS-32602 Indoor Play © Frank Schaffer Publications

CLASSROOM MANAGEMENT

Physical education should be a positive experience for the teacher and the students. Teaching activities indoors should not be any more difficult than teaching on the playground. The key to a successful lesson is establishing and maintaining control of the classroom. Making students aware of the rules and the expectations for indoor activities will help ensure that everyone enjoys an exciting, well-ordered learning experience.

BOUNDARIES

The first step toward maintaining order indoors is to set the boundaries. The boundaries should be defined for the students at the beginning of each lesson. The most obvious boundaries are the walls themselves, but walls alone are not sufficient. The students must also be aware of what areas of the room are available to them. There must be clear expectations given as to what equipment, furniture, and space is within their boundaries.

ESTABLISHING TEAMS

The next step in successful indoor classroom management is to pre-establish teams for the students. The way in which this is done can vary according to class level. The teacher's leadership is essential in this process to ensure that the *playing* time is not overcome by the *planning* time.

It is important for the instructor of **primary** levels to take charge of setting up the teams in order to save valuable playing time. When the instructor establishes the teams, he or she can create a good gender balance on the teams and equally disperse the students with more athletic ability among the teams.

For the teacher of **middle** levels, it is possible to allow the students to choose their own teams as long as selections are made in a fair and equitable manner. If this is not possible, have students "count off" by number. (For example, 15 students could count off by threes to create five groups.) Then you may choose or the class may vote on team captains.

Another method for teachers of any level to use in establishing teams in the classroom is to use existing table groups or cooperative groups as teams.

Once the teams are established, give each team a number or allow the teams to give themselves team names. Keep the same team numbers or names from month to month, but shuffle students around to create new teams!

ROUTINES

To ensure that indoor physical education classes progress efficiently, it is important to establish easy-to-follow routines. At the beginning of each class, the students should line up with their teams for warmup exercises. The teacher should begin the warmup by leading the students in some type of aerobic activity such as jumping jacks or jogging in place. Next, with the students standing an arm's-length distance apart from one another, the teacher should lead the students in stretching exercises. Older students may also lead these exercises. Appropriate warmup and stretching exercises are described on pages 9–15.

After the warmups and stretches are completed, the teacher should explain and model the skills that the students will practice for the lesson. Skill practice is an important component of the physical education program and should be completed before the students engage in games or structured activities. After the students have had time to practice skills, they can then participate in the planned game or activity for the day. At the conclusion of the day's lesson, have the students once again line up with their teams before being dismissed or returning to other classroom activities. If time permits, have the students do a few stretching exercises.

SIGNALS

It is important to implement an indoor quiet signal. When used sparingly, a whistle can serve as an effective signal in a gymnasium or multipurpose room. Other effective indoor signals include a clapping pattern or a hand signal, such as a "V" salute. The students should be trained to stop, look at, and listen to the teacher as soon as the signal is given. If the students are spread out over a large playing area in a gymnasium or multipurpose room, they should be instructed to come in and line up in front of the teacher when they hear or see the signal. Students who do not respond to signals should be disciplined according to the teacher's indoor classroom management plan.

DIRECTIONS

The instructor must give clear and explicit directions for every activity so that the students know what is expected of them. He or she should then check for understanding by asking the students to repeat the directions. While explaining directions verbally, the teacher must be sure to model expected behaviors and skills for each activity.

FS-32602 Indoor Play © Frank Schaffer Publications

CREATING A LESS COMPETITIVE ATMOSPHERE

One of the most important ingredients for a successful fitness program is a noncompetitive atmosphere. Physical education class should not be about winning and losing. Nor should it be a time in which some students feel intimidated, while others become overly competitive. It should be a time when all students can feel safe and secure with themselves and their own ability levels.

To achieve this atmosphere, the teacher should choose activities that are appropriate for the average skill level of the entire class. An instructor can build students' self-esteem by setting all students up for success and praising them for their efforts. One way a teacher can set up the students for P.E. success is by avoiding activities that are too difficult for the less-skilled students. If students feel confident about their abilities, they will all be more inclined to participate actively.

In order to manage competitiveness, the teacher should not allow the teams to keep score while playing games. The teacher can praise and reward individual students for such things as teamwork, positive attitudes, good sportsmanship, and effort instead of acknowledging winning teams. Giving continual positive feedback to the student during every activity and presenting awards to students for positive efforts models appropriate sportsmanship behaviors. (See pages 118–126 for achievement awards and progress forms.)

SAFETY

Another important management consideration is how to ensure the students' safety. When planning P.E. activities, consider the safety precautions that must be taken to prevent injuries and accidents. The students should be told to come to school in appropriate clothes for participating in physical education. They must wear rubber-soled shoes and loose, comfortable clothing that their parents know may get dirty. The playing area must be checked to ensure that it is free of obstacles such as wastebaskets, chairs, tables, and audiovisual equipment, or breakable objects. It is crucial for the teacher to maintain control of all activities throughout the lesson in order to ensure a safe environment. Finally, any physical challenges that the students may have, such as asthma, vision and hearing problems, scoliosis, or physical injuries must be taken into account when planning and implementing a lesson.

TIME

The use of time is another important management strategy. Limit the warmup and stretching segment of the class to between 5 and 10 minutes. Transition times between activities should take less than one minute. Explaining and modeling the skills for the activity should not exceed 5 minutes. Allow 10 to 20 minutes for the game or activity. Finally, allow a few minutes at the end of each lesson for the students to cool down and get drinks of water. Overall, each lesson should last from 25 to 40 minutes.

Because students enjoy testing their own speed, it is also helpful to use a stopwatch to time how fast the class can respond to specific instructions, such as lining up or putting equipment away. Giving the students time frames for performing tasks is an extremely effective management tool. Have them practice these skills and challenge them to reduce the time spent on specific tasks.

SPACE

There is often insufficient space for physical activity. It is important, therefore, to plan ahead for each indoor lesson to be sure that there is adequate space for the activity. In the classroom, furniture may have to be rearranged or incorporated into the activity. If the activity will take place in a gymnasium or multi-purpose room, it is important to check the room ahead of time to be sure that the lesson space is clear and adequate.

FS-32602 Indoor Play © Frank Schaffer Publications

AVOIDING PROBLEMS

Avoiding potential problems before they happen will lead to successful lessons. It is imperative that the teacher maintain control of the class at all times. The games should not be allowed to become overly competitive, and the students should be cautioned to follow directions at all times. Students who do not get along should be placed on different teams. A student who loses control should take a short time-out away from the class. The use of the gymnasium or multipurpose room should be coordinated among all the teachers to avoid overcrowding and the resulting confusion. Whenever possible, the room should be set up ahead of time with boundaries marked and equipment and furniture arranged as needed. Routines and your discipline policy must be consistent.

It is important to choose activities that actively involve the entire class. The teacher should plan enough variation and activity into the lesson so that students spend little—if any—time sitting and waiting for an opportunity to participate. Keep everyone involved and moving as much as possible. One way to ensure continuous student participation is to keep the activities fast-paced and orderly. Music is another great way to keep students interested. There are many activities, such as relay races and aerobics, that can be enhanced with upbeat music to help motivate the students.

Finally, the teacher should be enthusiastic about physical fitness in general and about the activities in particular. The teacher should model skills and should participate in activities when appropriate. The teacher who gives students a love for physical activity and fitness will truly give them a gift for a lifetime.

EQUIPMENT

Having the proper equipment is another key to managing the indoor classroom. A whistle and a stopwatch are important pieces of equipment for the successful physical education program. Careful planning will ensure that the necessary equipment is ready for each lesson. It is convenient to have the required number of materials in a sturdy bag or on a small cart with a whistle, stopwatch, and paper and pencil for noting both achievement and discipline problems. Storing all P.E. materials in a separate closet or cupboard will make keeping track of the equipment easier. It is essential to keep an inventory of P.E. materials and to be sure that the equipment is in good repair and properly marked.

A good imagination is invaluable when it comes to acquiring equipment. It is not necessary to purchase brand new, and often expensive, equipment. If you are on a tight budget, try to solicit equipment donations. Parents may be willing to donate new or used sports equipment. Tennis and racquetball clubs may donate used equipment in good condition. Even major sporting good companies may respond favorably to a letter requesting donations and discounts on new equipment.

Equipment
- stopwatch
- Hula-Hoops
- whistle
- handballs
- parachutes
- soccer balls
- tennis balls
- plastic cones
- jump ropes
- whiffle or foam balls
- beanbags
- balloons
- classroom supplies such as wastebaskets, paper, pencils, erasers

FS-32602 Indoor Play © Frank Schaffer Publications

WARMUP

As an introduction to each lesson, it is important that the students participate in warmup and stretching exercises. These components of the program are important not only for instilling lifetime skills and habits, but also for preserving students' health and safety. It is imperative that students learn to warm up their bodies and stretch their muscles before exercising in order to help prevent injuries.

It is important—and fun—to vary the type and amount of warmup activities the students perform. The directions below and on the next page describe indoor exercises that will warm the students' muscles without overtaxing the available space.

JUMPING JACKS

Jumping jacks are a time-honored conditioning exercise that build endurance and increase coordination. Students stand behind their desks with their feet together and arms at their sides. Then, they jump to a position with their legs slightly more than shoulder-width apart and their arms extended overhead so that their hands touch. Last, the students jump to their original positions. The entire three-step process should be performed as a continuous movement. Students can complete up to 20 jumping jacks as a warmup.

JOGGING

In the classroom, students can jog in place for one or two minutes to warm their muscles and build endurance. In the gym or multipurpose room, students may jog slowly around the room's perimeter.

For added fun—if space permits—the students can be told to change the direction in which they are jogging when they hear a whistled or clapped signal. The students will begin by jogging in one direction, and then when they hear the signal, they must reverse their direction and jog the other way.

KICK-BACKS

In a gymnasium or multipurpose room, students can add kick-backs to their warmup repertoire. Kick-backs are fun four-count exercises that begin with the students standing up straight with their arms at their sides. On the count of *one*, the students squat down and touch the ground with both hands out in front of their bodies. On the count of *two,* they keep their hands on the ground and kick both feet out behind them. On the count of *three,* they bring their feet directly under their bodies so that they return to a squatting position. On the count of *four,* they stand up, completing one kick-back. The class can perform 5 to 10 kick-backs as a warmup activity. They should perform this exercise in unison, calling out the count of each full kick-back as it is completed.

ABDOMINAL CRUNCHES

Although abdominal crunches do require enough space for a student to lie on his or her back with legs bent, a particularly spacious classroom might accommodate this exercise. They make an ideal warmup in a gymnasium or multipurpose room. Abdominal crunches are a form of sit-ups that differ from the traditional sit-ups in that, when performed correctly, they cause less stress on the lower back. The students should begin by lying on their backs with their legs bent. Interlocking their hands behind their heads, the students should slowly lift their shoulders up off the ground. The students should raise their shoulders only five or six inches before lowering them to the ground. Raising the shoulders and torso any higher can cause pain or injury to the lower back. The first several times the students perform abdominal crunches, they should "crunch" only five times per session. As their form and strength improve, they can be encouraged to increase the number of crunch repetitions.

FS-32602 Indoor Play © Frank Schaffer Publications

STRETCHING

After the warmup exercises, the class should perform at least 10 stretches each day covering the major muscles of the body. Each stretch should be held for 10 to 15 seconds while using the correct form. The entire class should perform the stretches together. The teacher should model each stretch and perform it with the class. When working with older students, the teacher can select one or two students to lead the class in the daily stretching routine. If the students have been separated into squads or teams, a different squad can lead the warmup and stretching activities each day.

SUGGESTED DAILY STRETCHES

Standing Quadriceps Stretch

Stand on one leg with the knee slightly bent. Hold the opposite foot with one hand, and pull the heel toward the buttocks. After 10 seconds, switch legs and repeat on the other side.

Hip Flexor Lunge

Stand with one foot in front of the other, toes pointed forward. Bend the forward knee 90 degrees and extend the rear leg back, lowering the hips toward the ground. After 10 seconds, switch legs and repeat on the other side.

Calf Stretch

Stand with one foot about one foot in distance in front of the other. Keep the heel of the back foot on the ground while leaning the weight forward onto the front foot. Hold for 10 seconds, switch legs, and repeat.

Hamstring Hang

Stand up straight with feet together. Slowly reach down toward the ground with both hands while keeping the legs straight. Reach down as far as possible to feel a comfortable stretch. Hold for 10 seconds.

Crossover Stretch

Stand up straight and cross one leg over the other, keeping the legs straight. Slowly reach down toward the ground with both hands, and let the arms hang for 10 seconds. Slowly stand up, switch legs, and repeat.

Butterfly

Sit on the ground with feet together and knees bent in the front of the body. The bottoms of the feet should be touching each other. Slowly bend the upper body down toward the feet, while holding on to the feet with both hands. Bend down to a comfortable stretch, and hold it for 10 seconds.

Straddle Stretch

Sit on the ground with straight legs spread out as far as comfortably possible. Slowly reach out with both arms toward the left foot and hold the position so that the chest is flat out over the legs in a comfortable position. Hold for 10 seconds and repeat on the right side. Repeat a second time reaching arms straight out in front of the body.

Sit and Twist

Sit on the ground with the legs straight out in front of the body. Take the right leg and cross it over the left leg, and place the right foot on the ground, keeping the knee bent. Slowly turn the body to the right side and place the left elbow on the outside of the right knee. Hold for 10 seconds and repeat on the other side.

FS-32602 Indoor Play © Frank Schaffer Publications

Cross Chest

Stand up straight with feet together. Reach the right arm straight across the chest. Place the left hand on the right elbow and pull the right arm into the body. Hold for 10 seconds and repeat with the other arm.

Overhead Reach

Stand with feet shoulder-width apart and knees slightly bent. Place the right hand on the right hip and lean to the right. Extend the opposite arm overhead and reach to the right. Hold for 10 seconds. Repeat by leaning to the left side.

Knee Hug

Lie flat on the ground with the knees bent and feet flat on the ground. Slowly bring the right knee up toward the chest and hold for 10 seconds. Repeat with the left knee. Slowly bring both knees toward the chest, lift up the head toward the knees, and hold for 10 seconds.

Sit and Reach

Sit on the ground with the legs straight out in front of the body. Slowly reach out with both hands and hold on to the ankles, with the chest and head as close to the legs as comfortably possible. Hold for 10 seconds.

Triceps Stretch

Stand up straight with feet shoulder-width apart. Lift one arm overhead with the elbow bent and close to the head. Grasp the elbow with the opposite hand and pull back slightly. Hold for 10 seconds, switch arms, and repeat.

Shoulder Rolls

Stand up straight with feet shoulder-width apart and arms straight down at the sides. Slowly raise the shoulders up toward the ears, then rotate them backward and down to the starting position. Repeat four times. Reverse the rotation direction so that the shoulders rotate forward, and complete five repetitions.

Arm Circles

Stand up straight with feet just beyond shoulder-width apart. Extend the arms out to the sides, and keep them parallel to the floor. Keep the arms straight and move them slowly to create small clockwise circles. Continue the motion while gradually creating larger circles. Reverse the direction, and beginning with large counterclockwise circles, slowly move to smaller circles. Continue the circles for 30 seconds, changing directions as needed.

Neck Stretches

Stand up straight with feet shoulder-width apart, and place hands on the hips. Keep the chin up, look toward the right, and hold for 10 seconds. Turn the head, look toward the left, and hold for 10 seconds. Repeat turning and looking to each side three times. Next, slowly lower the right ear toward the right shoulder and hold for 10 seconds. Then slowly lower the left ear toward the left shoulder and hold for 10 seconds. Repeat to each side three times.

Seated L

Sit on the floor with one leg straight out in front of the body. Bend the other leg so that the bottom of the foot is touching the inside of the straight leg. Slowly reach out with both hands toward the foot of the straight leg and hold for 10 seconds. Switch legs and repeat on the other side.

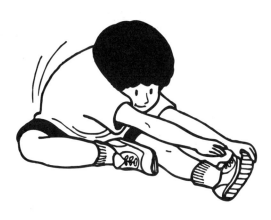

Squat

Stand with the feet shoulder-width apart and the toes pointed out to the sides. Slowly squat down while keeping the feet flat on the ground. Keep the knees to the outside of the shoulders. Hold for 30 seconds.

Back Stretch

Lie flat on the floor with straight arms extended over the head. Slowly reach as far as possible in opposite directions with the arms and legs. Hold for five seconds, relax, and repeat.

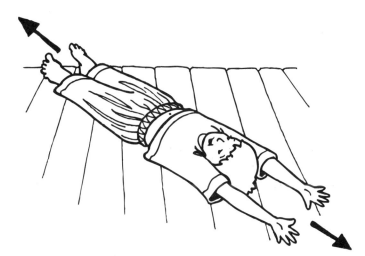

Cross-leg Stretch

Sit on the floor with the legs crossed over each other. Slowly lean forward and reach out with arms extended as far as possible. Hold in a comfortable position for 10 seconds.

FS-32602 Indoor Play © Frank Schaffer Publications

CLASSROOM PLAY

GAMES AND ACTIVITIES FOR THE CLASSROOM

Physical education does not end just because the weather keeps the class indoors. When no other space is available, it is possible to have a well-rounded fitness program inside the classroom. The essential requirements for such a program are motivation, flexibility, and creativity.

Each lesson should begin with the same warmup and stretching routine that is used in a gymnasium. The only difference is that it may be necessary to move the furniture around. Be aware of any possible safety issues that may exist in the classroom. Think about what is involved in each activity and adjust the room as needed.

Go into each classroom activity with a positive attitude. The students need to be reminded that it is possible to have their P.E. time inside the classroom and still have fun.

Be flexible at all times. Have more than one activity planned for each class period. Sometimes the games go by more quickly than anticipated; other times they don't work with your classroom arrangement. Be ready to switch to a different game or activity at any time. Often, simply modifying a game will make it a successful activity in a given situation.

This chapter will cover a variety of indoor games and activities that can be used in the classroom. They require very little equipment and setup time. Most important, they will allow your students to be actively involved in fitness activities without leaving the room.

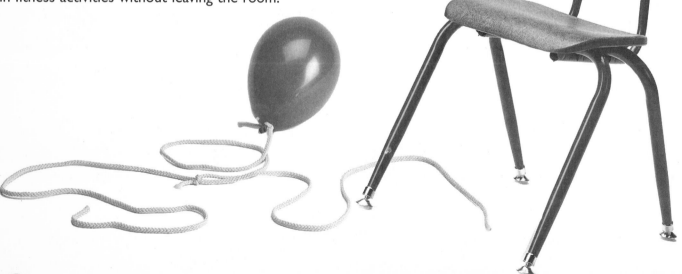

FS-32602 Indoor Play © Frank Schaffer Publications

Animal Two by Two

This activity encourages students to use their imaginations as they imitate animal movements and look for other students who are imitating the same animal.

EQUIPMENT
- one 3"x5" index card per student

GETTING STARTED:

Before beginning the activity, make two identical sets of animal cards by writing the name of a different animal on each pair so that there are two cards for each animal and one card for each student. Make a third card for one animal in the event that there are an odd number of students. Choose animals that will be easy for the students to imitate such as a bear, a dog, a kangaroo, a rabbit, a penguin, an elephant, a cat, a bird, a duck, or a monkey. For younger students, it may be necessary to paste a picture of the animal on the card. Arrange the desks so that there is a large open space in the room. Have the students stand around the perimeter of the open space.

RULES:

Explain to the class that each student will receive a card with the name of an animal written on it. He or she must move around the room while imitating the movements of that animal whose name appears on the card. As each student moves about the room, he or she must look for another student who is imitating the same animal. When a student finds his or her animal mate, the partners must stand together until everyone has found a mate. Collect the cards and start again. The students may not trade cards, and they must perform movements for the animals on their cards.

SAFETY PRECAUTIONS
Make sure the students stay within the open space and do not run around the room.

Beanbag Pitch

This activity encourages students to practice their eye-hand coordination by throwing beanbags at a target.

EQUIPMENT
- one beanbag per group, one small box per group

GETTING STARTED:

Arrange desks in traditional, linear rows. Place a box on the front desk of each row so that the box opening faces toward the other desks in the row. Place the beanbags on the last desk in each row. Divide the class into groups of four to six students.

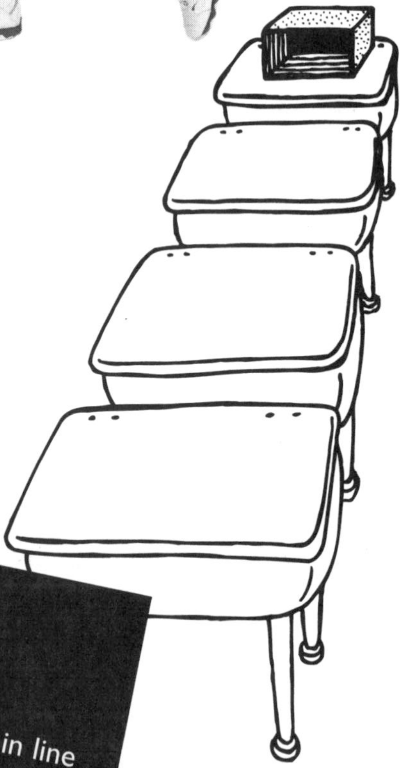

RULES:

Each player has three consecutive chances to stand behind the row of desks and throw the beanbags in an attempt to land the beanbag inside the box. The last player in each line will retrieve the beanbag for the thrower. The thrower will become the beanbag retriever after completing his or her third toss. The initial retriever will return to the end of the line. One point is scored for each beanbag that lands completely inside the box. Scores are kept for each player and then added to the team's total after each team member has taken a turn. Each team must keep its own score. The team with the highest score wins. As a variation, give the students a time limit in which to score a certain amount of points.

SAFETY PRECAUTIONS

The students should remain in line while waiting for their turn. Use only one beanbag per group.

Chair Aerobics

Aerobics activities can be easily modified so that students may get the fitness benefits of regular aerobics while seated in their chairs.

EQUIPMENT
• music (optional)

GETTING STARTED:

If possible, have the students move their chairs several feet away from their desks. Begin the warmup period with slow music, if available. Lead the students through stretching exercises, beginning with the legs and slowly working up to the arms. Remember to hold each stretch for at least 10 seconds. Consult the stretching section of this book for examples.

PROCEDURE:

After four or five minutes of stretching, switch to faster music and lead your students through the following chair exercises. Conclude with a brief cooldown period by having the students walk slowly around the room several times and then perform several stretching exercises.

SAFETY PRECAUTIONS
Allow for as much room as possible for students to work freely. Caution students to stop exercising immediately if they feel lightheaded or dizzy.

- Hold the bottom of the chair with both hands and raise alternate knees up and down.
- Reach down to the floor with the left hand and then the right hand.
- Hold the bottom of the chair with both hands and alternate lifting each leg straight up to seat level and down again.
- Stand in front of the chair and place the hands on either side of the chair. Raise the right leg backwards straight up and down 10 times, and then repeat with the left leg.

Chair Ring Toss

In this game, students attempt to toss rings onto the legs of an upside-down chair.

EQUIPMENT
• one chair for each group, five plastic or rope rings per group

GETTING STARTED:

Move the desks to the sides of the classroom to create a large open space. Have each group take its chair and turn it upside down on the floor so that the legs face the group. Divide the class into groups of three to five students, and distribute a set of rings to each group.

RULES:

Each team must line up 10 feet away from its chair. Each player will take a turn at throwing the rings (one at a time) at the legs of the chair. Players score 10 points for each ring that lands on the back legs of the chair and 5 points for each ring around the front legs of the chair. Allow the students to play several rounds. As a variation, give each team a challenge of scoring a certain amount of points within a given time frame.

SAFETY PRECAUTIONS
Spread out the chairs so that the teams will not be in each other's way. Make sure the chairs are balanced while they are upside down.

FS-32602 Indoor Play © Frank Schaffer Publications

Concentration

This is a simple circle game in which the students will have to respond to a given number or perform a fitness task.

EQUIPMENT
- none needed

GETTING STARTED:

Arrange the furniture so that there is a large open space in the room. Have the students sit in a circle.

RULES:

Instruct the students to count off around the circle starting with the number one, and tell them that they must remember their numbers. When working with younger students, prepare a series of index cards with one number on each card. Give a card to each student for use as a memory jogger. Ask each student to repeat his or her number. The game begins with one student, chosen by the teacher, calling out a random number. The person whose number is called must immediately call out another number. If the student significantly hesitates, he or she will perform five abdominal crunches. (An abdominal crunch is a modified sit-up in which only the head and shoulders are lifted off the floor.) The student then calls out a new number and the game continues.

Vary the activity by giving each student a letter of the alphabet or a number in a pattern, such as 2, 4, 6, 8, 10, etc. The fitness activity can also be changed for each round.

Ducks Fly

This is a wonderful activity for younger students, as it involves imagination and listening skills.

EQUIPMENT
• none needed

GETTING STARTED:

Have the students stand next to their desks. Randomly choose a leader.

RULES:

The leader will stand in front of the class and call out "Ducks fly." The students must now begin to flap their wings. The leader will continue to call out animals by saying, for example, "Birds fly" or "Crows fly." As long as the leader calls out an animal that flies, the students will continue flapping their wings. If the leader says the name of an animal that does not fly, for example, "Dogs fly," the class should stop flapping their arms. Students who are caught flapping their arms must sit down. Choose a new leader after every four or five animals have been called out. The round continues until only four or five students are standing. Choose a new leader and play again until everyone has a turn at being the leader.

Beanbag tag

Beanbag tag improves students' coordination as they move about the room.

EQUIPMENT
- two beanbags

GETTING STARTED:

No advanced preparations are required.

RULES:

Have students remain at their seats, and choose one person at random to be "It." Give this student two beanbags. He or she must balance one beanbag on his or her head and then start to walk around the room holding the second beanbag. The student must place the beanbag he or she is holding on another student's desk. As soon as the beanbag is placed on the desk, the second student must stand up, balance the beanbag on his or her head, and chase the "It" student without running or dropping the beanbag. "It" will try to circle the room and reach the second student's seat before being tagged. If a beanbag falls, the player must stop and replace it before continuing. If the "It" student is tagged, he or she will remain "It" and will receive the second beanbag and start again. If "It" successfully reaches the second player's seat, that player becomes "It."

SAFETY PRECAUTIONS

Make sure there are no obstacles on the floor.

Heads Up, Seven Up

This is a simple game of blind tag that takes place at the students' seats and involves the whole class.

EQUIPMENT
• none needed

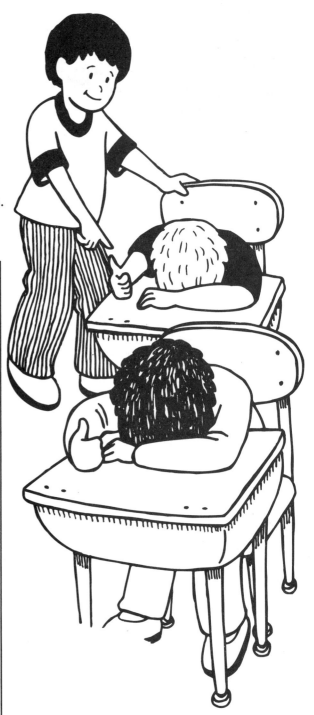

GETTING STARTED:

Have the students remain at their desks, and choose seven students to come and stand in a row at the front of the room. Appoint one student to be the leader of the group.

RULES:

Instruct the class that when the leader calls out, "Heads down, thumbs up," the seated students must put their heads down on their desks and hold their right thumbs up in the air. While the students have their heads down, the seven students at the front will walk around the class. Each of the seven students will quietly touch one person's thumb and then return to the front of the room. Students whose thumbs are tapped should immediately hide their thumbs in their fists so that they are not tapped again. The seated students may not look up while their heads are down. When all of the seven have returned to the front of the room, the leader will call out, "Heads up, seven up!" All of the students will sit up, and the ones who were tapped should stand. They will have an opportunity to guess who tapped them. If a student guesses correctly, he or she will take the tapper's place in the front of the class, and the tapper will sit down. If the tapper's identity is not guessed, he or she will remain at the front of the class. If a tapper is not identified after three rounds, he or she must be replaced with a new player.

FS-32602 Indoor Play © Frank Schaffer Publications

Hide the Beanbag

In this fun activity for large groups, children take turns hiding beanbags and searching for them among their group members.

EQUIPMENT
- one beanbag

GETTING STARTED:

Clear a large area in the center of the classroom. Have students sit scattered around the open space.

RULES:

Choose one student to stand in one corner of the classroom with his or her eyes closed. This student will be the searcher. Give the beanbag to a randomly chosen student and have him or her sit on the beanbag so that it cannot be seen. Have the searcher walk among the seated students to look for the beanbag. The rest of the students will give the searcher clues to finding the beanbag by clapping. They will clap softly when the searcher is far away from the beanbag and will clap more loudly as the searcher gets closer to the beanbag. At any time, the searcher may tap a student on the shoulder if he or she thinks that the student is hiding the beanbag. The searcher can tap up to three students in an attempt to find the beanbag. If the searcher fails after three tries, the hider should reveal the beanbag. Begin a new game.

Hot Balloon Potato

In this game, which can be played with any number of players, students can develop their reflexes and listening skills as they pass a balloon around the group.

EQUIPMENT

- one balloon per group, music, stickers

GETTING STARTED:

Arrange the furniture so that there is a large open space in the room. Organize groups of 5 to 10 students into circles, and give each group a balloon.

RULES:

When the students hear the music play, they must pass or hit the balloon around the group. When the music stops, the person left holding the balloon will receive a sticker. Keep playing until everyone has several stickers.

SAFETY PRECAUTIONS

Be sure students do not try to hit the balloon out of each others' hands.

It's a Draw!

Students take turns drawing sports- or fitness-related objects on the board while their classmates guess the objects.

EQUIPMENT
- chalkboard and chalk or white board and markers

GETTING STARTED:

Divide the class into four teams. Give each team a marker or piece of chalk.

RULES:

Have each team send an artist to the chalkboard to draw an object associated with sports and fitness. Tell the teams' artists first what to draw. The teams will try to guess what the object is in order to receive a point. The artist may not talk or give body-language hints. Every person must have the chance to draw. The first team to recognize and call out the name of the object earns one point. Then have another artist from each team draw an object. Continue until a team earns 10 points and wins the round. If time permits, continue play until every student has had a chance to draw.

Keep It Up

Level of difficulty: simple

This game is played with groups of six to eight. It is a simple activity involving balloons and cooperation.

EQUIPMENT

- one balloon per group, music (optional)

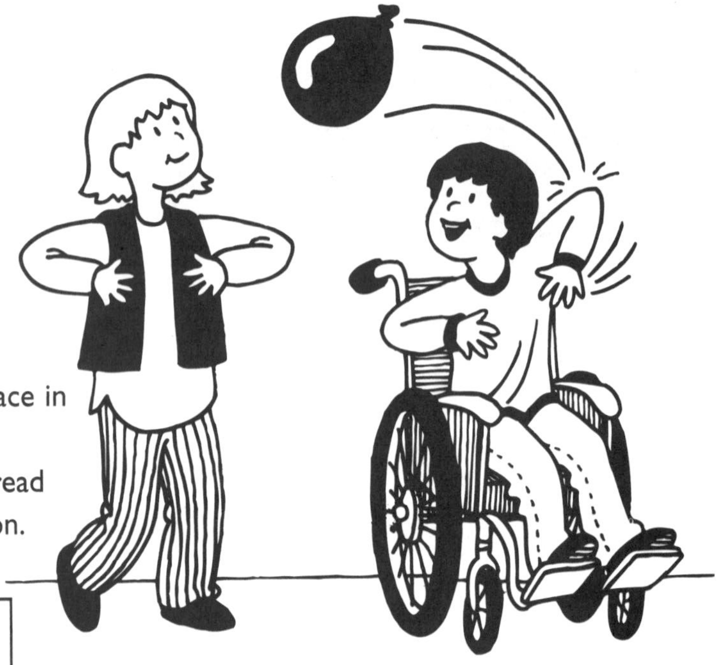

GETTING STARTED:

Arrange the furniture so that there is a large open space in the room. Divide the class into groups of six to eight students each. Arrange the groups into circles, and spread the circles around the room. Give each group a balloon.

RULES:

At a signal, such as turning on music or blowing a whistle, have students in each group use their hands, feet, heads, shoulders, or knees to keep the balloon in their group from hitting the floor. They must stop when they hear the signal again. In subsequent rounds, change the rules. For example, have the team members hold hands while keeping the balloon up or allow the students to use only their elbows.

SAFETY PRECAUTIONS

Spread the teams far enough apart so that they will not run into each other. Do not allow high kicking.

Limbo

Students try to walk underneath a limbo stick placed at various heights without knocking the stick down.

EQUIPMENT

• several long sticks such as yardsticks or broom handles, music (optional)

GETTING STARTED:

Arrange the room so that there is a large open space. Begin by turning on some upbeat music.

RULES:

Choose two students of essentially equal height to hold up the stick. Have them place it on the open palms of their hands at shoulder height to start. The students will form a line and one by one will try to walk underneath the stick without knocking it over. Students may touch the stick, but they may not touch the floor with their hands. If a student knocks the stick over, he or she is out. Have the students who are out begin a new limbo game in another area of the classroom.

After each student has gone under the stick, choose two new students to hold the stick, and have them hold it at a lower height as classmates limbo beneath it. Repeat this process by continuing to lower the stick until only one player is left. Start over, and challenge the students to see how low they can go.

SAFETY PRECAUTIONS

Be sure that the students have sufficiently stretched their muscles before participating in this activity.

Match, No Match

In this activity, students move around the room while trying to make a match with a partner.

EQUIPMENT
- none needed

GETTING STARTED:

Arrange the furniture so that there is a large open space in the room.

RULES:

Instruct each child to find a partner and then stand together back to back. Tell the students that when the teacher calls out the word *same*, they must turn around and face their partners while holding up either one or two fingers. If both partners are holding up the same number of fingers, it is a match. If the partners are holding up a different number of fingers, it is no match. Students may not change their fingers after they turn around. The partners who made a match will hold their fingers up in a V to represent victory. The no-match partners must now move around the room and find new partners from the no-match pool. The game will begin again when everyone in this group has a new partner.

Over-the-Shoulder Relay

Level of difficulty: **simple**

This is a simple relay that can be played either at the students' desks or using a minimal amount of classroom open space. It is played in teams of five or six.

EQUIPMENT
- six objects per team (use items such as beanbags, balls, and erasers)

GETTING STARTED:

Divide the class into teams of five or six players. Have the teams stand in single-file lines facing the front of the room. Hand the six items to the first player in each line.

RULES:

When you give the signal to begin, the first player will pass each of the items one at a time over his or her left shoulder to the second player in the line. The second player must have all six objects before passing them on to the third player, and so on. When the last player in line has received all of the objects, that player will call out to the group to turn around and face the opposite direction. The relay will now continue in the same fashion, but in reverse. The first team to successfully pass all of the objects back to the first player wins the relay.

Paper Ball Shuffle

This is a silent cooperative game played in groups of four at the students' desks using paper balls.

EQUIPMENT
- one paper ball per group

GETTING STARTED:

Arrange the desks into groups of four so that the students will be facing each other with their desks pushed together. Each group of four students will be a team. Give each team a paper ball.

RULES:

The object of the game is to keep the paper ball moving around the tops of the desks for as long as possible. The team members must pass the ball around the desks without talking and without the ball falling on the floor. If the ball falls on the floor or a person talks, the team cannot score any points. Each round will last for a specific amount of time and will be worth more points as the time limit increases. Start the first round with a 20-second time limit worth only one point. Increase each round so that the students are eventually working toward keeping the ball moving silently for up to five minutes and at a value of 20 points.

FS-32602 Indoor Play © Frank Schaffer Publications

Rain

Level of difficulty: simple

The teacher leads the class in this classic activity in which the students use their hands to simulate the sound of a rainstorm.

EQUIPMENT
• none needed

GETTING STARTED:

Divide the class into three groups.

PROCEDURE:

Explain to the students that when you stand in front of one of three groups, the group members must imitate the motion you are performing. They will continue to perform the motion until you return and show them a different motion. Instruct the students not to speak so that they can hear the rain-like sounds created by their hands.

Stand in front of the first group and rub your hands together. Slowly walk past each group until all the students are rubbing their hands together. Repeat this step two more times but with different hand movements, such as snapping your fingers and slapping your hands on your thighs.

Next, return to the first group and rub your hands together. Move to the second group and snap your fingers. Move to the third group and slap your thighs. While each group is performing a different motion, return to the first group and slap your thighs. Slowly walk past the remaining groups while performing this motion. Then walk past the groups while snapping your fingers.

Finally, return to the first group and rub your hands together. Then walk past the remaining groups until everyone is performing this motion. Stand in front of the entire class as you continue rubbing your hands together. Slowly stop this last motion. The rainstorm is over.

FS-32602 Indoor Play © Frank Schaffer Publications

Ready, Set, Show

This activity combines math with a physical activity. Students work in pairs to solve math problems that are based on the number of fingers each student puts up.

EQUIPMENT
- none needed

GETTING STARTED:

Arrange the furniture so that there is a large open space. Divide the class into pairs, and have the pairs spread out around the open area.

RULES:

Each pair of students will stand back to back. Each student will display a number using his or her fingers. The first partner will say "ready," the second person will say "set," and the first person will say "show." Tell the students that on "show" both partners will turn around and show their numbers. They must quickly add the numbers together. The first partner to call out the answer will win the round. The winner will perform two jumping jacks, and the loser will perform four jumping jacks. The winner of each round will start the next ready, set, show chant.

Increase the level of difficulty according to the grade level. For younger students, have them use simple addition of the numbers 1 through 5. Allow older students to show numbers up to 10. For the upper grades, instruct the students to multiply the numbers.

FIVE!

Smile If You Love Me

This old favorite with younger students involves trying to make classmates smile.

EQUIPMENT
• none needed

GETTING STARTED:

Arrange the furniture so that there is a large open space in the room. Have the students form a large circle, and place one student in the center of the circle.

RULES:

The object of this game is for the student in the center to make another student smile while those around him try to keep from smiling. The student in the middle will choose any other student, stand directly in front of him or her, and say, "Smile if you love me." The center student can also make funny faces, but he or she may not touch the classmate. In response, the circle member must try to keep a straight face. If this child does not smile, he or she will remain a part of the circle. If the child does smile, he or she must join the center student in trying to make someone else smile. The game continues until everyone is smiling.

Squeeze a Ball

This simple activity helps develop the students' hand strength and ball-passing skills.

EQUIPMENT
- several small, dissimilar rubber balls or racquetballs

GETTING STARTED:

Select several small rubber balls that are easily identifiable. Arrange the furniture to create a large open area. Have the students form a circle, and distribute the balls to two or three students around the circle.

RULES:

The students will begin by passing each ball to the right. They will squeeze the balls with their right hands before handing them gently to their neighbors. The balls may not be thrown. When a ball returns to where it started, have the student squeeze it with his or her left hand and then pass the ball to the left.

Three-Object Relay

This cooperative relay takes place at the students' seats and involves passing three objects in a specified pattern.

EQUIPMENT
- three objects (such as beanbags, erasers, or small balls) per row

GETTING STARTED:

Arrange the desks so that they are in rows.

RULES:

The teams will consist of all the students in two adjacent rows. Each student will turn his or her chair to face the student across the aisle. Place the three objects on the desk of each student at the front of the rows. When you give the start signal, the first student in each row will begin to hand the objects across the aisle to the second person in the next row, who will then hand the objects to the third person on the other side of the aisle. This pattern will continue down the aisle and back to the front again. Students may not throw the objects, and they must follow the given pattern. Each round ends when all three objects have returned to the first person.

For younger students, start the relay with only one object and add the second and third objects when the students have become proficient at completing the pattern.

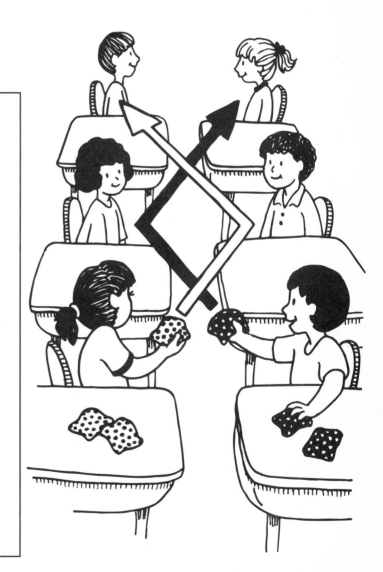

Thumb Wrestling

This is a simple, fun, nonviolent activity in which two students use only their thumbs in a wrestling match.

EQUIPMENT
• none needed

GETTING STARTED:

Instruct the students to find a partner and then stand in an open space. Explain that the partners will be participating in a thumb-wrestling exhibition. Choose one pair to stand in front of the room to demonstrate the activity.

RULES:

The two students will stand face to face. Each student will raise his or her right hand in a fist to chest height with the thumb up. Next, the students will interlock their fingers while keeping their thumbs raised. The object of the game is to completely push the other student's thumb down. The match begins when the partners count to three and then say "go." Once the students have had several minutes to practice with one partner, announce that they will begin switching partners after each match. Partners may agree to use their left hands during any given match.

SAFETY PRECAUTIONS

Be sure that the students do not pull each other's hands and do not become aggressive with their hands.

Wastebasket Relay

This cooperative relay involves passing objects down the rows of the classroom, as well as students changing seats in order to complete the relay.

EQUIPMENT
- one object (beanbag, eraser, tennis ball, paper ball, etc.) per student, one wastebasket or box per team

GETTING STARTED:

Arrange the desks into equal rows. Each row of students will work together as a team. Place one object for each player on the team on the first desk in the row. Place a wastebasket or box on the floor in front of the first desk in each row.

RULES:

When you give the students the signal to begin, the first student in each row will pass one object over his or her shoulder to the student seated behind. This will continue until the object has reached the last student in the row. When the last player receives the object, he or she will get up, walk to the front of the row, and place the object in the wastebasket. Once the object is in the basket, all of the players on the team must stand up and move to the desk directly behind them. The player who placed the object in the basket will sit in the first seat and will then pass an object from the desk to the second player in the row. This procedure will continue until all of the objects have been placed in the wastebasket. Students may not throw the objects or run to the front of the row.

SAFETY PRECAUTIONS
Strictly enforce the no-running rule.

FS-32602 Indoor Play © Frank Schaffer Publications

Balloon Basketball

This is a safe, indoor version of basketball that uses a small amount of space and balloons as basketballs.

EQUIPMENT
- one round balloon per student, two wastebaskets or boxes

GETTING STARTED:

Move the furniture to the side of the room so that there is a large empty space in the center of the room. Place the wastebaskets side by side at one end of the room. Divide the class into two teams. Have the teams line up single file at the opposite end of the room from the baskets. Assign one wastebasket to each team. Give a balloon to the players at the front of each line.

RULES:

At a signal, have the players at the front of each line begin walking toward their respective teams' baskets. Remind the players to keep the balloons moving in the air as they travel toward their baskets. Tell the players to try to hit their balloon into their team's basket. When a player scores a basket, give the next player in line a balloon and have him or her move toward the basket. Caution students not to interfere with players on the other team. Continue until each person has completed the task. The first team to hit all of its balloons into its basket wins. After declaring a winner, start a new game.

SAFETY PRECAUTIONS

Clear a large playing area. Make sure there are no obstacles in the way.

FS-32602 Indoor Play © Frank Schaffer Publications

Balloon Volleyball

Volleyball is a great game for outdoors or the gym, but it can also be easily modified for classroom play. Using balloons and string, groups of four students can safely practice beginning volleyball skills in the classroom.

EQUIPMENT

- five-foot length of string per group, two-foot length of string per group, at least one balloon per group

GETTING STARTED:

Divide the students into groups of four. For each group, tie a two-foot length of string to an inflated balloon. Tie the other end of the string to the center of a five-foot length of string.

RULES:

Each end of the five-foot length of string is held by a student at waist-height. The remaining two players will stand on either side of the string and will bat the balloon back and forth across the string. Instruct the students to hit the balloon with their right hands. After two minutes, have them use only their left hands to hit the balloon. In following rounds, have the students kick the balloon first with their right feet, then with their left feet. Have extra balloons available in case a balloon breaks. Allow the students to switch positions frequently.

SAFETY PRECAUTIONS

Do not allow the students to hold the balloons near their mouths or faces.

FS-32602 Indoor Play © Frank Schaffer Publications

Dice Baseball

This is a fun way to play baseball in the classroom without balls and bats. The students use dice while moving around the room to designated bases.

EQUIPMENT
- one die per game, chalkboard, chalk

GETTING STARTED:

Divide the class into two teams. If there are more than 24 students and enough space in the room, it is advisable to play two games simultaneously. Arrange the desks so that there is a large open space. Place four chairs in a diamond fashion in the middle of the open space to look like a baseball field. Have the two teams sit at opposite sides of the room. Choose one student on each team to act as captain. This student will give each teammate a number, which will serve as his or her place in the batting order. Designate one team to be at bat. The other team will keep track of the outs and the score on the chalkboard.

RULES:

Each batting team will get three outs before giving up the die to the other team.

The batter will take the die and roll it on top of the home plate chair. The baseball value for each roll of the die will be played as follows:

1 = single   2 = double   3 = triple   4 = home run   5 = out   6 = out

The student will look at the number and play the outcome. If the batter rolls a one, he or she will walk to first base and sit down. If the player rolls a two, he or she will walk to second base and sit down, and so on. Each player will remain on base until a roll of the die forces him or her to advance to another base. Each player will come to bat in turn as designated by the batting order. There will be only one throw of the die for each batter.

If the batter rolls an out, the player must wait for his or her turn to come up again. After three outs, any players on base must return to their team and the other team will roll the die. All teams must remain seated until their turn at bat. After each team has come to bat one time, one inning has been completed. Nine innings make up a complete game.

Football Scramble

This game uses football terminology and involves the entire class in an active seat-changing game.

EQUIPMENT
• none needed

GETTING STARTED:

Use the existing classroom setup for this game. The students may sit on top of their desks. Give each student in the class one of five football positions: quarterback, wide receiver, fullback, center, or tight end. Distribute the positions evenly and randomly. Designate one student to start the game as the leader.

RULES:

The leader will call out one of the positions. All of the players with that position must stand up and change seats with one another. The leader must also try to find a seat, so the players must move quickly, but without running. The one person left standing becomes the new leader and calls out the next position. Make sure that all of the positions are called out more than once.

SAFETY PRECAUTIONS

Strictly enforce the no-running rule. Make sure that there are no obstacles in the aisles.

Group Juggling

This activity, which is done in groups of five or six, helps develop students' eye-hand coordination and thinking skills as they juggle crushed paper balls.

EQUIPMENT
- three or four crushed paper balls per group

GETTING STARTED:

Before beginning the activity, crumple sheets of paper into tight balls. Arrange the furniture so that there is enough open space for several groups to stand in circles. Divide the class into groups of five or six students, and assign each group one of the open areas around the room. Have the groups stand in circles, and give each group one paper ball.

RULES:

Have the students begin by passing the ball around the circle to the left. After a minute, instruct the students to stop and change the direction of the ball so that it is going to the right. In the next round, have them throw the ball across the circle. The ball may not be thrown hard or above the receiver's neck. When the groups have become proficient at these tasks, create a more difficult pattern. For example, have the students throw the ball to the student two persons to their right. Continue to give the groups new patterns. After the groups spend sufficient time working with one ball, add another ball to the circle so that the students are completing the pattern with two balls. Continue to add balls until each group is juggling up to four or five balls in a given pattern.

SAFETY PRECAUTIONS

Insist that the balls be thrown in a safe, friendly manner. Be sure to separate the groups as much as possible.

Human Tic-tac-toe

In this game, students play Tic-tac-toe by using their bodies as the X's and O's.

EQUIPMENT
• nine chairs per game

GETTING STARTED:

Arrange the chairs into three rows of three. Divide the class into two equal teams. (Use two separate games for larger classes.) Assign one team to be the X's and the other team to be the O's.

RULES:

Each team will take a turn at placing a member in a chair until one team has placed three players in a row either down, across, or diagonally. Allow teams to huddle together to make decisions, or permit each player to choose where to sit. After each game, all of the players must return to their teams, and different players must have a chance at sitting at the tic-tac-toe "board." You can help younger students visualize the game more clearly by providing players with X and O signs.

Pass and Duck

Level of difficulty: moderate

This is a fun ball-passing relay that can be played in the aisles of the classroom with teams of five or six.

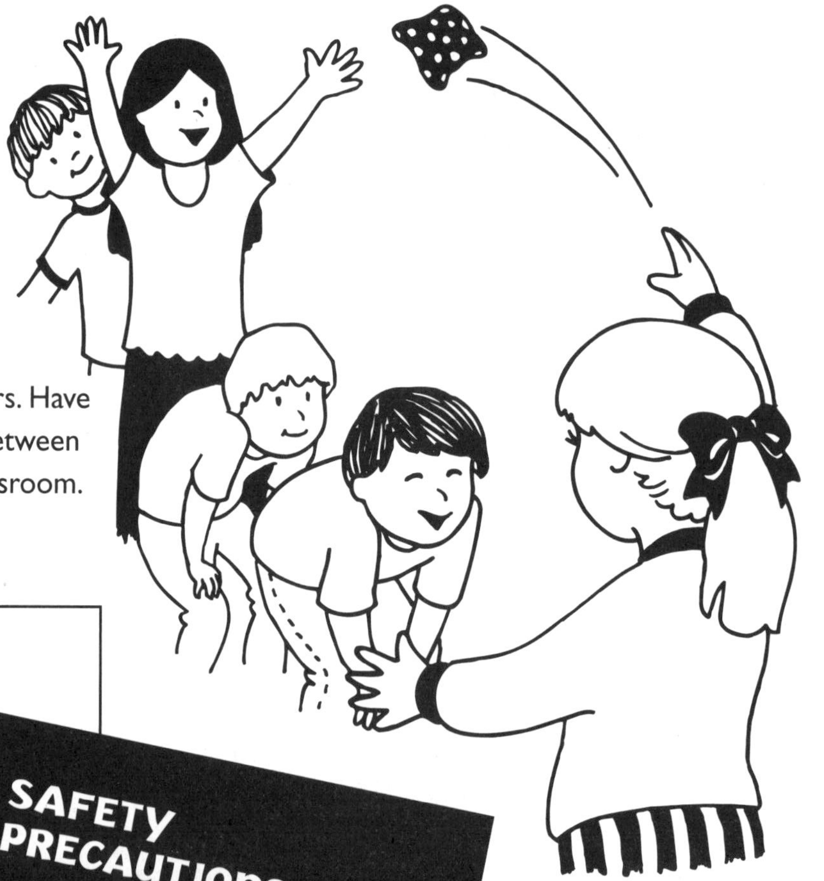

EQUIPMENT

- one small ball or beanbag per team

GETTING STARTED:

Divide the class into teams of five or six players. Have each team stand in a line either in the aisles between the desks or in another open space in the classroom. Give the first student on each team a ball.

RULES:

The player with the ball (the thrower) will take three steps forward, turn around, and face his or her team. The thrower will pass the ball to the first person in line, who will then pass it back. The first player will then duck down. This player, and all subsequent players who duck, must stay down until a new student becomes the thrower. The ball will then be thrown to the second player, who will throw it back and duck. This pattern will continue until the last player has received the ball. This player will go to the front of the group to become the next thrower, and the original thrower will go to the front of the line. This will continue until the team has returned to its starting positions.

SAFETY PRECAUTIONS

Be sure that the desks do not interfere with the walking path of each team. Do not allow players to run at any time.

Silent Speedball

This is a simple ball-passing game that can be played with the students standing beside their desks.

EQUIPMENT
- **one small foam ball**

GETTING STARTED:

Instruct the students to stand beside their desks. Begin the game by throwing the ball to a player at random.

RULES:

The object of this game is to catch the ball without dropping it and to make accurate tosses to classmates. Each player has three seconds in which to toss the ball to another player. The toss must be made so that the target player can easily catch the ball. If the ball is tossed over the person's head, or bounces off the furniture, the thrower is out and must sit down. If the catcher drops the ball, he or she must sit down. The round ends when there are only two people left standing.

Variations: Add rounds in which the students must ask a question when throwing the ball and the catcher must catch the ball and give the correct answer in order to stay in the game. For example, use multiplication facts so that the thrower must give a multiplication problem such as 9 x 5, and the catcher must give the correct answer of 45 within three seconds to stay in the game. Other rounds could involve state capitals, word opposites, addition problems, or anything else that students should be able to answer in a short amount of time.

SAFETY PRECAUTIONS

Use a soft ball made of either foam or vinyl. Strictly enforce the rule against hard or erratic throws.

FS-32602 Indoor Play © Frank Schaffer Publications

GYM OR MULTIPURPOSE ROOM PLAY

GAMES AND ACTIVITIES FOR THE GYM OR MULTIPURPOSE ROOM

Gymnasiums and multipurpose rooms can provide enough space for a class to engage in many different types of fitness activities, cooperative games, and movement activities.

When planning lessons for the gym, make sure that the room is available during the time in which you wish to use it. Bring all of the necessary equipment or check to see that everything needed is easily accessible in the gym. Also check the room out ahead of time, and remove any furniture or equipment that will interfere with the lesson. If there are gym mats available, be sure that they are laid out before the lesson.

Start each activity with the proper warmup and stretching activities. Plan each lesson in advance, and allow extra time for getting to and from the classroom. Also remember to keep the students involved and active throughout each lesson. When it's possible and practical, incorporate existing gym equipment into some of the lessons.

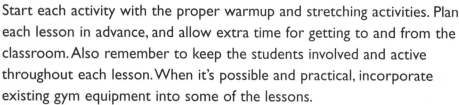

Individual Fitness Activities

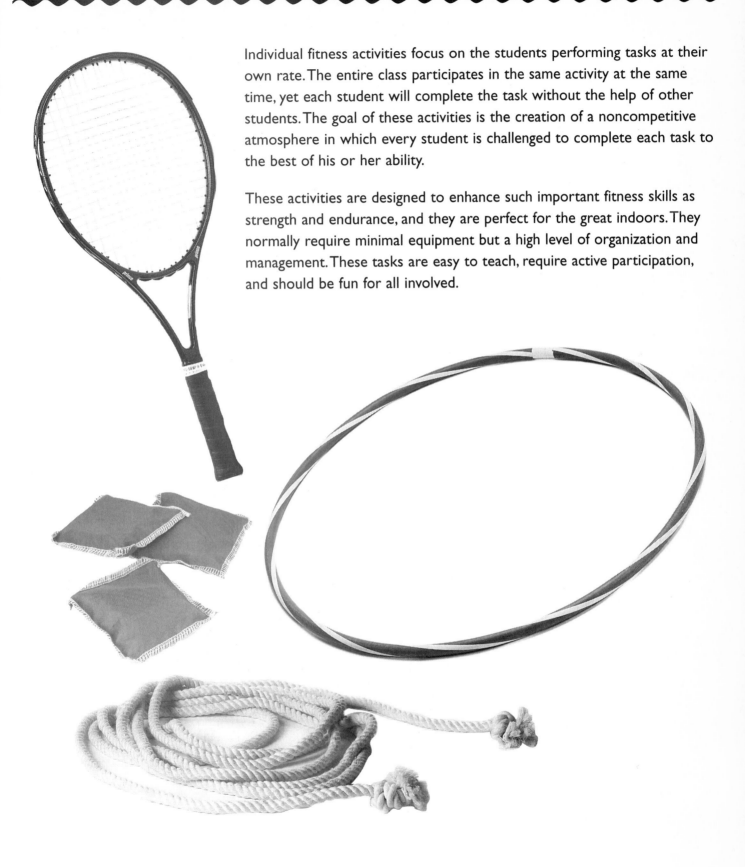

Individual fitness activities focus on the students performing tasks at their own rate. The entire class participates in the same activity at the same time, yet each student will complete the task without the help of other students. The goal of these activities is the creation of a noncompetitive atmosphere in which every student is challenged to complete each task to the best of his or her ability.

These activities are designed to enhance such important fitness skills as strength and endurance, and they are perfect for the great indoors. They normally require minimal equipment but a high level of organization and management. These tasks are easy to teach, require active participation, and should be fun for all involved.

FS-32602 Indoor Play © Frank Schaffer Publications

Beanbag Balance

This activity for younger children involves balancing a beanbag on one's head while performing movement skills.

EQUIPMENT
• one beanbag per student

GETTING STARTED:

Distribute a beanbag to each student. Have the students form two lines at the back of the room while holding their beanbags in their hands.

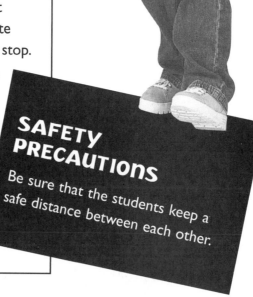

RULES:

Instruct the students to place the beanbags on their heads. When you give them the signal to begin, the students will start walking around the perimeter of the room. They must stay in their lines and keep the beanbags in place without using their hands. After the students complete one trip around the room, give the signal to stop. Explain that each time they hear your signal, they will be instructed to move in a different way. At various intervals, instruct the students to skip, hop, speed up, slow down, walk backwards, walk on their toes, or walk very low to the floor. If a student drops a beanbag, he or she will pick it up and place it back on his or her head.

SAFETY PRECAUTIONS

Be sure that the students keep a safe distance between each other.

FS-32602 Indoor Play © Frank Schaffer Publications

Bunny Hop

This is a fun hopping activity for younger students that can be set to music.

EQUIPMENT

- recording of "The Bunny Hop" song (if available), audio player

GETTING STARTED:

Explain to the students that they will be learning how to hop like a bunny. Have the students spread out around the room and face you.

PROCEDURE:

Demonstrate the dance steps, remembering to keep your knees slightly bent. The students will tap their right heels one time out to their right, and then bring their feet in. They will repeat this step. Next, they will tap their left feet out to their left, bring their feet in, and repeat. Lastly, they will hop forward three times. Help them to practice all of the steps several times. When the students become proficient with all of the steps, have them join in one long line to perform the dance together. Have them stand one behind the other with their hands on the shoulders of the person in front of them. Now the students are ready to dance to "The Bunny Hop" song (if it is available).

SAFETY PRECAUTIONS

During practice, be sure there is enough space between students to avoid collisions.

Connect the Dots

Level of difficulty: **simple**

This is a modified version of an obstacle course in which the students move around the room according to numbered dots on the floor while performing various movement skills.

EQUIPMENT
- paper, masking tape, whistle

GETTING STARTED:

Before beginning, draw large connect-the-dots-style numbered dots on sheets of paper (one per student), and tape them to the floor in numerical order. Place a masking-tape starting line near the first dot. Instruct all of the students to line up behind the starting line.

RULES:

When you blow the whistle one time, everyone must freeze. When you blow the whistle twice, the students must move to the next dot. Each person must proceed to the next number in order. Vary the whistle blows so that the students must listen carefully. Continue the activity until everyone has completed the course. For variation, have the players perform a particular movement skill through the course—hopping, skipping, jumping, or crawling to each number.

SAFETY PRECAUTIONS

Spread out the course around the room, but make sure that consecutive numbers are in the same area.

FS-32602 Indoor Play © Frank Schaffer Publications

Hop to It

In this easy pattern activity, the students perform various hopping exercises in order to develop their jumping and coordination skills.

EQUIPMENT
• none needed

GETTING STARTED:

Organize the students so that they are standing in rows and are an arm's length from their nearest classmates.

RULES:

Instruct the students to hop on one foot. About 30 seconds later, have them switch to the other foot. Next, direct them to hop in numbered sequences so that they hop once on each foot, then two times per foot, then three times, etc. Then give them more complicated patterns, such as hopping once on the left foot and then twice on the right.

After the students have tried several hopping patterns, challenge them to see how high off the ground they can hop. Next, have them hop on one foot in a circle. Then have them increase the height of their hops each time they hop around the circle. Finally, choose several of the hopping tasks from the following list or create your own:

- hop forward, backward, and to the side
- hop while holding the free foot
- hop lightly, then heavily
- hop for distance
- hop out the shape of letters or numbers on the floor
- create a hopping sequence.

SAFETY PRECAUTIONS
Be sure that there is sufficient space between students to avoid collisions.

FS-32602 Indoor Play © Frank Schaffer Publications

Obstacle Courses

Obstacle courses can easily be created in any situation to provide the students with an opportunity to develop an array of skills such as jumping, skipping, and balancing.

EQUIPMENT

• items such as Hula-Hoops, jump ropes, cones, beanbags, balls, wastepaper baskets, chalk or tape, low balance beam, bats, and plastic flying disks (Frisbees)

GETTING STARTED:

Before beginning the activity, gather all of the available equipment and plan a course that is appropriate for the given grade level. Establish a starting line with a cone or a line on the floor. From this point, spread out obstacles around the room in a given direction, and designate a finish line. Vary the types of obstacles and tasks. Be creative, but always consider the safety of a given task.

RULES:

The students must perform the tasks as designed. Possible tasks could include the following:

SAFETY PRECAUTIONS

Be sure that the tasks are not too difficult for the age level.

- jumping over jump ropes
- running through a series of cones
- stepping or hopping in and out of hoops
- walking on a low balance beam
- throwing a beanbag or ball through a hoop or into a wastebasket
- crawling under a table
- jumping rope a given number of times
- standing a bat perpendicular to the ground, placing the forehead on the handle, and spinning around three times
- twirling a hoop a given number of times
- spinning a plastic disk on the ground

Snow Play

This is a fun cold-weather activity for younger students, who exercise their bodies and their imagination while pretending to play in the snow.

EQUIPMENT
- none needed

GETTING STARTED:

Have the students spread out around the room.

PROCEDURES:

Tell the students to imagine that they are out in the snow. Have them close their eyes and picture themselves in the snow. Help them to envision how the snow looks, feels, and smells. Instruct them to open their eyes and feel the cold. Tell them to act out what it would feel like to be very cold. Next, have them stomp their feet and move around the room as though they are walking through deep snow.

Then instruct the students to make imaginary snowballs. If they have not experienced this before, guide them through the steps of picking up imaginary snow and packing it together into a tight ball. Allow them to make several snowballs and even a snowman. After several minutes, start a snowball fight by throwing an imaginary snowball at a student. Encourage everyone to join in.

Finally, have the students lie on their backs on the floor with their feet together and their hands by their sides in preparation for making snow angels. Describe each movement and have them act out the descriptions. Start by instructing them to open their legs wide and bring them back together several times. Next, tell them to sweep their arms up toward their heads and back to their sides several times. Finally, have them imagine and describe what the snow would look like when they were finished.

SAFETY PRECAUTIONS

Keep the snowball fight under control so that students do not accidentally hit each other.

Stop and Touch

This is an excellent eye-foot coordination activity for younger students that involves moving and controlling a ball with the feet.

EQUIPMENT
• one small ball per child

GETTING STARTED:

Have the students spread out around the room and place a ball at the feet of each child.

RULES:

When you give the signal, each student will move a ball around the room by pushing it with his or her feet. When you give the command to stop, each child will place a foot on top of the ball. Remind the students not to stand on the ball, but merely to place a foot gently on it to keep it from moving. Allow them to practice this skill several times. Next, have them stop the ball with the other foot. When they have become proficient at stopping the ball with each foot, add a new challenge. This time tell them to stop the ball with another body part, such as a hand, a knee, or an elbow. Repeat this activity several times.

SAFETY PRECAUTIONS

Instruct the students to move around the room in the same direction.

Swimming

In this movement and imagination activity for younger students, the children make a splash in their make-believe swimming pool.

EQUIPMENT
- gym mats (if available), tape or cones, beachball (optional)

GETTING STARTED:

Place the gym mats in a large rectangular shape in the center of the room. (If necessary, use tape or cones to mark off the "swimming pool.")

PROCEDURES:

Have the students stand around the perimeter of the pretend pool. Tell them to imagine that it is a hot day and they will all be able to go swimming in the school's pool. Instruct them to dip a toe in to test the water temperature. Is it hot or cold? Have the students indicate the temperature through body gestures. Then let them jump in and splash around.

Next, instruct the students to lie on their stomachs and swim, remembering to kick their legs and move their arms in a swimming motion. After a minute or so, have them roll onto their backs to swim the backstroke. After a minute of this, tell them that they will take a break by floating on their backs. Instruct them to lie very still with their arms and legs straight. Then challenge them to swim on their sides or to invent their own strokes.

As a variation, the students may "swim" around the area while walking. They will move in the correct direction according to each stroke. For extra fun, let the student bat a beachball in the pool.

SAFETY PRECAUTIONS

Remind the students that there should be no horseplay in the pool. Be sure that the students maintain enough space between one another so that there will be no collisions.

Aerobics

The exercises featured in this aerobic workout not only strengthen the students' muscles but will also improve their cardiovascular fitness by accelerating their heart rates. This activity can be personalized to suit the fitness level of your students.

EQUIPMENT
• music (if available)

GETTING STARTED:

Have the students spread out in a large area. Explain to the students that you will be leading them in aerobic exercises and that they must follow along with you. The lesson should be divided into three sections: 1) warmup, 2) aerobic workout, and 3) cooldown.

1. Warmup: Use music to encourage the students' right-from-the-start participation in warmup activities. Begin this section with slow music. Lead the students through stretching exercises that begin with the legs and work up gradually to the arms. Remember to hold each stretch for at least 10 seconds. Consult the stretching section of this book for examples.

2. Aerobic Workout: After 5 minutes of stretching exercises, the students will be ready to move. Switch to livelier music, and start the aerobic section by having the students jog in place. Instruct them to pump their arms as they jog. This speeds up their heart rates and warms up their muscles. Now lead the students in performing exercises from the list below. Each movement should be executed for 30 to 60 seconds. This section should last from 5 to 20 minutes depending on the age and ability level of the class. Remind students that they should be in constant motion.

   The following recommended exercises are all appropriate for the full aerobic section of the lesson. Feel free to add movements. If time permits, go back and repeat movements.

   • Do jumping jacks with arms only.

   • Do jumping jacks with legs only.

   • Do full jumping jacks.

- Begin with arms at sides, then bring them up to the chest and back down.
- Raise both arms so that hands are at neck level, extend arms straight up into the air, and bring them back down.
- Punch both arms straight out in front of the body.
- Punch alternating arms straight up in the air.
- Hop in place with both feet.
- Hop on one foot.
- Stand on one leg and swing the other leg back and forth, then alternate legs.
- Keep both arms straight and swing them back and forth.
- Lunge forward by taking a step with one leg and bending the forward knee; then stand up, step back, and lunge forward with the other leg.
- Raise both arms so that elbows are at chin level. Squeeze elbows together, then move them apart.
- Hold both arms straight out to the side, bring them together in front of the body, then move them back out to the side.
- Bend from the waist to the side and reach down toward the ground with a hand. Repeat back and forth on each side.
- Kick one leg straight up in the air, then kick with the other leg.
- Kick each leg while swinging the opposite arm.
- Bring both elbows up over the head. Extend hands straight up in the air, keeping elbows in by the head.
- Stand with both legs straight, raise up on the toes, hold this position for five seconds, then slowly lower the heels to the floor.
- Alternate lifting knees while touching each knee with the opposite elbow.
- Alternate lifting knees while touching each thigh with both hands as it rises.
- Bounce up and down on the balls of the feet.

FS-32602 Indoor Play © Frank Schaffer Publications

3. Cooldown: Return to slower music to begin the cooldown period. Have the students walk slowly around the exercise area. Instruct them to take long steps and swing their arms slowly. After one minute, lead the students in cooldown stretches. Tell them to stretch their arms high above their heads and raise up on their toes. Then have them bend at the waist to one side and then to the opposite side. Next, instruct the students to lie flat on their backs and stretch their arms over their heads. Then have students bend one knee, pull it to the chest, and then stretch it up straight in the air. Repeat with the other leg. Finally, have the students squat in a crouched position with their hands at their ankles. Now instruct them to slowly roll their bodies up until they are standing up straight with their arms at their sides.

SAFETY PRECAUTIONS

Allow for enough room for students to work freely. If a student becomes short of breath, instruct him or her to walk slowly around the perimeter of the room for several minutes. If the child is still out of breath, have him or her sit down. Be aware of any health problems, such as asthma, that the students may have. Caution students to stop exercising immediately if they feel lightheaded or dizzy.

FS-32602 Indoor Play © Frank Schaffer Publications

Basic Tumbling and Movement

Level of difficulty: **simple to moderate**

The students will practice basic tumbling and movement skills while working in groups of five or six.

EQUIPMENT
• gym mats

GETTING STARTED:

Place the gym mats so that they form a large square covering as much of the gym floor as possible. Have the groups line up side by side and sit down at the end of the mats. Explain to the students that they will be learning and practicing basic tumbling skills. If possible, have a second adult on hand to help support the students' necks as they tumble.

TUMBLING AND MOVEMENT SKILLS:

Demonstrate each skill yourself. Then have one student from each group step onto the mats. Explain that the students will perform the skill repeatedly until they reach the end of the mats; then they will return to their groups. Each student must sit in line while awaiting his or her turn.

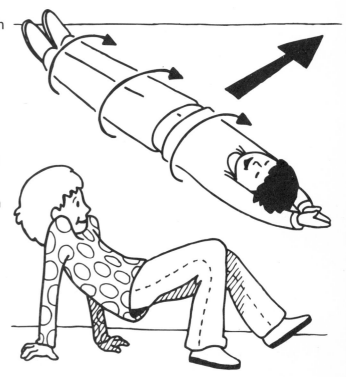

1. Logroll—The students will lie on the mats with their bodies straight and their arms over their heads. They will roll themselves to the end of the mat and back again. They should take as much time as necessary to roll straight and avoid veering into one another.

2. Crab Walk—The students will walk backwards with their hands behind their bodies and their feet in front of them. They begin by sitting with their backs toward the mats. Next, they place their hands next to their hips while their feet are flat on the floor in front of their bodies. They will push themselves up with their hands and then start traveling. Remind the students to turn their heads periodically to see where they are going.

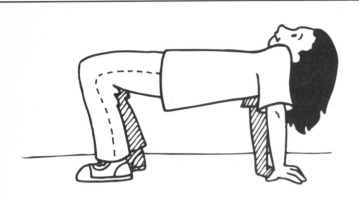

3. Table—The students will sit with their feet flat on the mats in front of them and their hands on the mats beside their hips. They will then push their hips up into the air while straightening their arms and keeping their knees bent so that their thighs and upper bodies are as flat as tables. Instruct each student to make a table, hold it for five seconds, move back several feet, and repeat the movement until he or she has reached the end of the mat.

4. Bridge—This is a similar skill to the Table; the difference is in the placement of the hands. To make bridges, the students will start by lying on their backs with their hands flat on the mats, their fingers next to their ears, and their feet flat on the ground. They must push themselves up with their hands and feet so that their backs are arched. Each student should make a bridge, hold the position for five seconds, move back several feet, make another bridge, and continue this pattern until he or she reaches the end of the mat.

5. Forward Roll—The students will start by kneeling down and placing their hands on the mats in front of their shoulders. Next, they will tilt their heads down so that their chins are touching their chests. Finally, they will use their feet to push their legs over their heads so that they will roll over. Be sure that they keep their heads down as they roll over.

FS-32602 Indoor Play © Frank Schaffer Publications

Fitness Challenge

This activity provides the students the opportunity to challenge themselves and to work at their own pace at individual fitness skills.

EQUIPMENT

- one Fitness Challenge Form (page 123) per student, five cups of pencils, jump ropes, pull-up bar, two stopwatches, tape measure, gym mats

GETTING STARTED:

Before beginning this activity, copy enough Fitness Challenge Forms for the entire class. It will also be helpful to set up the individual fitness stations in advance. The room should be arranged so that the following five stations are spread out around the room:

Station 1.   push-ups—Designate a small area.

Station 2.   abdominal crunches—Lay out gym mats if available.

Station 3.   jump rope—Place 5 to 10 jump ropes of various sizes in a large area.

Station 4.   pull-ups or chin hang—If available, use a built-in pull-up bar. (Arrange to have an adult aide on hand to assist with this station.)

Station 5.   long jump—Use masking tape to create a starting line and mark distances on the floor.

Place one cup of pencils at each station, and place one stopwatch at the jump rope station and the other stopwatch at the pull-up bar. Have the students sit down in the center of the room. Distribute the Fitness Challenge Form to each student in the class. Explain to the students that they will be participating in an individual fitness challenge. During the class period, they will be moving to each of the five stations, where they will be performing a fitness task and recording their results. Divide the class into five equal-sized groups. Send one group to each station.

RULES:

The students must move to each station in numerical order. Those groups that do not begin the challenge at Station 1 will go there after completing the Station 5 skill. Allow the students to move from station to station at their own rate as they finish each skill, but give a signal every five minutes to help the students pace their movement from station to station. Allow the students to take the fitness challenge several times during the school year so that they can try to improve their results.

Demonstrate the activities and familiarize your students with the procedures at each station:

1. Push-ups—The students will perform as many push-ups as possible. They may choose to do full push-ups on their hands and toes or modified push-ups on their hands and knees. They may make several attempts and record their highest scores.

2. Abdominal crunches—Abdominal crunches are similar to traditional sit-ups except that instead of raising their backs perpendicular to the floor, the students only lift their shoulders about six inches off the ground. The students should choose partners to help count for them. They may make several attempts and record their highest scores.

3. Jump rope—At this station the students will find jump ropes of several sizes and a stopwatch. All the students should take a minute or two to practice, and then one student will time the others to see how many times they can jump the rope in one minute. Choose several responsible students to help time the jump rope station. The timer will take a turn at jumping when a new timer arrives at the station.

4. Pull-ups or chin hang—The students may choose which of the two exercises at this station to perform. Students who choose pull-ups must pull themselves up so that their chins are above the bar for each pull-up. Students selecting the chin hang must hold their chins above the bar while being timed. It may be necessary for students to help boost one another up to the bar. Choose responsible students to time the chin hang. The stopwatch will be started when the student is already above the bar and should be stopped when the chin drops below the bar. In these exercises, the students must grip the bar with their palms facing them.

5. Long jump—The students may take three jumps and then record their longest jump. They must start with both feet just behind the line. They will propel themselves forward by swinging their arms and jumping. The distance will be measured from the starting line to the point at which the back of the jumper's heel touches the floor. The students should take turns jumping and measuring distances.

Juggling

Individual students learn and practice the basic skills of eye-hand coordination and concentration that are required for juggling. This activity should be practiced over several lessons.

EQUIPMENT
- three small balls (tennis balls, racquetballs, or beanbags) per student

GETTING STARTED:

Instruct the students to spread out around the room. Give each student one ball.

PROCEDURE:

Have the students practice tossing the ball up in the air with one hand and catching it in the other hand. Explain to the students that in basic juggling they should not catch the ball with the tossing hand. After allowing the students sufficient time to practice tossing one ball back and forth between the hands, give each student a second ball.

Have the students hold one ball in each hand. Explain that the next step to juggling is to learn how to toss two balls. Remind them that they should not catch a ball with the same hand with which they throw it and that the hands should never come together. Assure them that two-ball juggling is a difficult skill to master and will require practice. The students will toss the balls alternately in the air from one hand to the other. They should practice the rhythm of two-ball juggling, which is toss–toss, catch–catch. They will toss the ball from the right hand, then toss the ball from the left hand, catch the first ball with the left hand, and catch the second ball with the right hand. Allow ample practice time for this step. The students should become proficient with this skill before adding the third ball.

Three-ball juggling requires the same pattern of toss–toss, catch–catch, but a third ball is always in the air. The students will start with two balls in the right hand and one ball in the left hand. In order to be successful with three balls, they must be able to toss and catch balls continuously. This step takes a lot of concentration. Allow the students to work with a partner if they wish.

Students who master three-ball juggling can work on juggling two balls with one hand, which is a necessary skill for four-ball juggling. They will hold two balls in one hand and will alternately toss one into the air while catching the other. Instruct them to vary the height of the balls as they toss them.

SAFETY PRECAUTIONS

Be sure that there is ample space between students.

Cooperative Group Activities

Cooperative group games and activities are ideal for building cooperation and trust within any class. These activities place the students into small groups in which they must complete tasks requiring every type of fitness skill. The students must work together in order to complete the given tasks for each activity successfully.

There are no losers in cooperative activities. Students of every skill level will feel comfortable participating in these types of games. Every group completes the task at its own rate. The students will challenge themselves to perform at higher levels. They encourage one another and must cooperate, motivate, and respect each other in order to complete each activity. These activities are also designed to allow all of the students to experience success. To maximize the students' opportunities for success, be sure to choose activities that are appropriate for the skill level of your students.

Alphabet Ball

Level of difficulty:
simple

This is a simple activity for very young students that involves tossing a ball in a circle while reciting the letters of the alphabet or counting numbers.

EQUIPMENT
• one ball

GETTING STARTED:

Have the class form a large circle in the center of the room. Hand the ball to any student.

PROCEDURES:

The students will pass the ball around the circle. Allow them to practice passing the ball all of the way around the circle in one direction. Next, have them pass the ball around the circle in the other direction. Now they are ready to add the next task to the activity. Tell them that as they pass the ball around the circle, the person with the ball will recite a letter from the alphabet. The first person will start with the letter A, then pass the ball to the next person, who will say the letter B, and so forth.

To make it more difficult, start the ball around the circle with a random letter from the alphabet, and have the students continue from that letter. The students may also count out numbers in sequence. To make this more difficult, have the students recite a sequence of odd or even numbers.

Back to Back

In this partner activity, students use listening and cooperation skills while performing specific movement tasks.

EQUIPMENT

- whistle

GETTING STARTED:

Have the students spread out around the room.

PROCEDURES:

When you blow the whistle one time, the students must perform a given movement task, such as jogging, walking, skipping, or hopping. When you blow the whistle twice, each student must find a partner and stand back to back while waiting for the next instruction. After the partners are back to back, choose another skill for the students to perform. The students must choose a different partner in each round. For variation, have the students stand knee to knee, toe to toe, shoulder to shoulder, hand to hand, or head to head. If there is an odd number of students, allow one group to have three partners.

SAFETY PRECAUTIONS

Be sure that there is sufficient space between partner-groups to avoid collisions. Remind students that they must work cooperatively when performing the tasks with a partner.

Beachball Balance

Pairs of students work together to move the ball without using their hands in this easy and fun balancing activity.

EQUIPMENT
• one beachball per pair

GETTING STARTED:

Have each student find a partner, and give a beachball to each pair of students.

PROCEDURES:

Each pair of students must hold the ball between them without using their hands. Allow them to explore the different ways that they can accomplish this task. After several minutes, quiet the class and ask for volunteers to share the different ways that they can hold the ball between each other. They should be able to hold the ball stomach to stomach, head to head, side to side, back to back, and leg to leg. Next, have the students practice moving around the room while holding the ball in these positions.

When the students have become proficient at moving around with the ball, instruct them to form two lines at the back of the room. Have all of the groups move around the perimeter of the room at the same time, each holding the ball in the same fashion. At the end of one trip around the room, change the way that the pairs must hold the ball and begin again.

To make this more challenging, let the pairs try to hold two balls at one time, or have them move through an obstacle course.

SAFETY PRECAUTIONS

Be sure that there is sufficient space between the groups so that they can move safely.

Beanbag Tossing

In this simple activity for younger students, pairs of children work on their eye-hand coordination by tossing beanbags back and forth.

EQUIPMENT
- one beanbag per student

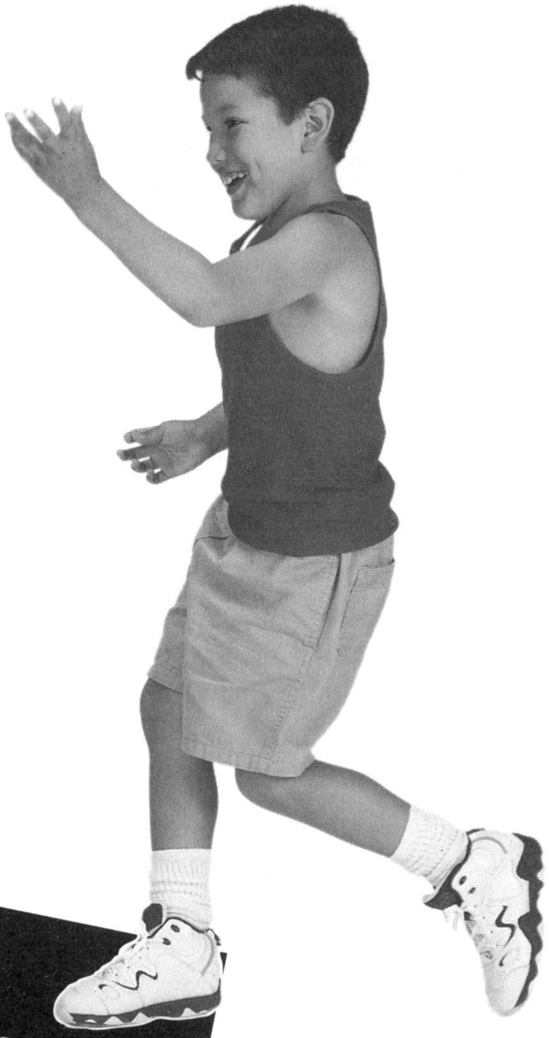

GETTING STARTED:

Have each student find a partner. Give each student a beanbag. Line up the partners so that they are facing each other across a short distance in two long rows at the center of the room.

PROCEDURES:

Instruct the students to pass one beanbag back and forth. Have them move back one step every minute or so as they become more proficient at throwing and catching. After several minutes of practice with one bag, have the students return to their original positions to toss two bags back and forth. Have them start with one partner tossing both bags simultaneously to the partner. Have them increase the distance between them as they get better at this task. Finally, challenge the partners to toss their beanbags at the same time.

SAFETY PRECAUTIONS
Be sure that there is sufficient distance between partner-groups to avoid collisions.

FS-32602 Indoor Play © Frank Schaffer Publications

Beat the Clock

This activity involves the entire class working together to perform tasks such as creating circles or letters with their bodies.

EQUIPMENT
• stopwatch

GETTING STARTED:

Prepare in advance a list of appropriate challenges for your class to perform. Select tasks that will force the students to work cooperatively. The number of challenges you can devise are as limitless as your imagination, but you may want to include the following ideas:

* one large circle with students holding hands
* two equal circles with students in each circle holding hands
* two circles, one inside the other
* two circles, one inside the other, each circle walking in a different direction
* one large square, rectangle, or triangle
* a given number of equal rows
* one large plus sign, multiplication sign, or division sign
* one straight line with students arranged from shortest to tallest
* one large letter such as T, H, or E
* numbers
* words
* simple math problems including numbers and signs

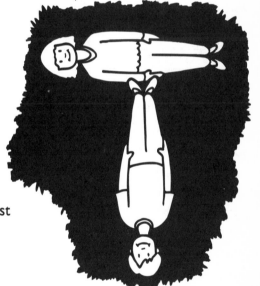

PROCEDURE:

Explain to the students that the class will be working together to solve challenges and that they must cooperate with each other to be successful. They will be competing against the clock in order to complete each task within a given amount of time. Challenge the students to repeat a task and attempt to reduce their time. Allow longer amounts of time for more difficult challenges such as creating numbers or math problems.

Group It

Level of difficulty:
simple

In this activity, the entire class works cooperatively to group itself according to a prescribed direction.

EQUIPMENT

- stopwatch

GETTING STARTED:

Prepare in advance a list of criteria students can use to sort themselves. Criteria for grouping students could include such things as eye color, hair color, month of birth, number of siblings, shirt color, favorite sport, and favorite food.

PROCEDURE:

Explain to the students that they will be working together to sort themselves into groups based on criteria you provide. Their goal will be to create each set of groups within a given amount of time.

Human Obstacle Course

This is a fun activity for younger students in which the students become the obstacles in a running course.

EQUIPMENT
- none needed

GETTING STARTED:

Explain to the students that they will be working together to create a human obstacle course. Ask the class what kind of obstacles they can create with their bodies. Help them come up with such ideas as cones to run around, obstacle to climb over, tunnel to crawl under, pole to spin around, etc. Then designate five to seven students to be the first group of obstacles.

PROCEDURE:

Place the human obstacles around the room, and help the students map out a route around the obstacles. Then start them on the course. The obstacles must remain stationary and may not touch the runners. Allow the first group of runners the opportunity to run the course several times, and then choose new students to be the obstacles. Continue this process until every student has had the opportunity to be an obstacle.

SAFETY PRECAUTIONS
Be sure to allow only obstacle positions that the runners can easily maneuver around.

Knee Wrestling

This is a modified form of wrestling in which partners try to score takedowns by tagging each other's knees.

EQUIPMENT
- whistle

GETTING STARTED:

Divide the class into pairs, and have them spread out around the room. The partners will face one another while standing two steps apart.

PROCEDURE:

The object of this game is to be the first player to tag a partner's knees three times. The students will try to move around their partners so as to tag their knees, while at the same time avoid being tagged themselves. When a person has reached three tags, he or she scores a takedown. As soon as a takedown is scored, the pairs will start a new game. Play each round for 30 to 45 seconds. At the end of each round blow the whistle. The partner with the most takedowns for the round will pair up with another winning partner. The remaining students will find new partners. As soon as everyone has a partner, begin a new round.

SAFETY PRECAUTIONS

In order to avoid collisions, be sure that the pairs have sufficient space.

Knots

Level of difficulty:
simple

In this fun challenge for groups of five to eight, students knot themselves together while holding hands and then unknot themselves without releasing their hands.

EQUIPMENT
• none needed

GETTING STARTED:

Divide the class into groups of five to eight students. Station the groups in widespread areas of the room. Have the students stand close together in their groups with both hands out in front of them.

PROCEDURE:

Each student will use his or her left hand to hold the right hand of any student who is not immediately nearby. Once everyone's hands are linked and the group is "knotted together," the students will begin unknotting themselves. To accomplish this task, they may not let go of one another's hands but may do anything else necessary to free themselves, such as crawl under, step over, or turn themselves around. Remind the students that this challenge takes time. They should not rush to untangle themselves.

The students will need cooperation, patience, and determination to unknot themselves. To increase the difficulty, add more players to the group and maybe even knot together the entire class.

Line Up Challenge

This is a fun and challenging whole-class activity in which students line up in a specific order.

EQUIPMENT
• stopwatch

GETTING STARTED:

Prepare in advance a list of various criteria students can use for determining their order in a line. For example, students could order themselves by age, by sex, by height, by birthday, by hair color, or by the number of siblings. Have the students sit scattered around the floor.

PROCEDURE:

Give the students specific directions on how they must line up. Challenge the students to line up as quickly as possible. Remind them that they will need to work cooperatively in order to succeed.

To provide an added challenge, time each task; then repeat the tasks at random and have the students try to beat their previous times. Test students' memory by having them repeat a task without talking.

Long Jump Challenge

This activity involves students combining the distances of their individual long jumps to see which group of four or five students can jump the farthest.

EQUIPMENT
• chalk or masking tape

GETTING STARTED:

Use chalk or masking tape to create a starting line at one end of the room. Divide the class into groups of four or five students. Line up the groups behind the starting line.

PROCEDURE:

The first student in each group will jump as far as possible and stay standing in the spot where he or she lands. The second student will start his or her jump from the spot where the first person landed. The third student will jump from where the second student landed, and so on. Students must stand beside their landing spots until the next student has jumped. The final student will hold his or her landing position until all the teams have completed their jumps. Declare a winner and start again. This time, challenge each team to beat its last total distance.

SAFETY PRECAUTIONS

Do not allow students to take a running start at their jumps.

79

Movement Patterns

In this activity, the class walks, hops, skips, and jumps around the room in patterns.

EQUIPMENT
• music (optional)

GETTING STARTED:

Have the students spread out around the perimeter of the room.

PROCEDURE:

Instruct the students to begin by walking 10 steps counterclockwise around the room. Signal for them to stop. Then add a new movement so that the students, for example, walk 10 steps and skip 10 steps. Allow them to complete the pattern two times. Then stop the class, and add a third movement to the pattern, reminding the students that they must perform each movement in the correct order.

Each time a movement is added, have the students orally repeat the entire pattern to check for understanding of the task. Slowly add more movements to the pattern without making the pattern too complicated for the grade level and ability of the class. As a variation, break the class into groups of five to eight students, and challenge them to create their own patterns. Invite each group to share its patterns with the class.

SAFETY PRECAUTIONS

Be sure the students are moving in the same direction and are sufficiently spread out around the room.

Musical Ball Pass

In this adaptation of musical chairs, groups of 10 to 15 students pass a ball around in a circle as music is played.

EQUIPMENT
- two medium-sized balls per group, music

GETTING STARTED:

Divide the class into groups of 10 to 15 students. Have each group stand in a circle facing the center. Give each group one ball.

PROCEDURE:

Instruct the students to begin passing the ball around the circle as soon as they hear the music start. When the music stops, the last student to touch the ball must go to the center of the circle. When the music begins again, the students will resume passing the ball to the person beside them. When the music stops, the last student to touch the ball will trade places with the student in the center of the circle. To make the game more challenging, add the second ball to each circle. There will then be two students in the center after each round.

FS-32602 Indoor Play © Frank Schaffer Publications

no-Net Prisoner

This is a modified version of the playground game of Prisoner and also a lead-in to playing volleyball.

EQUIPMENT
- chalk or tape, volleyball for every two teams

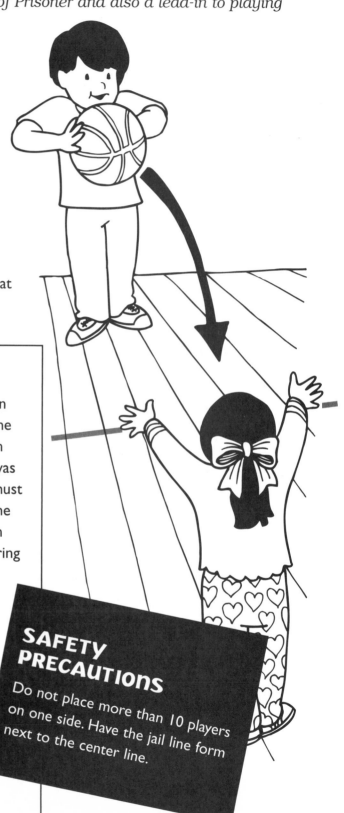

GETTING STARTED:

Create a line down the center of the room with chalk or tape (or use an existing line if playing in a gym). For each game, assemble two teams of 6 to 10 players. Have each team spread out over one side of the court. Make sure that the students know the names of everyone on the court.

PROCEDURE:

The player with the ball will call the name of a player on the other team and will then throw the ball over the line toward that team. Anyone on the other team may catch the ball. If the ball is dropped, the player whose name was called must go to prison, which means that he or she must stand off to the side of the court and form a jail line. The player who catches the ball will then call out a name on the opposite team and throw the ball over the net. During play, the ball must be thrown over the line and may not hit any walls, or else the thrower will be sent to jail. A team may free the first person in its jail line and get him or her back on the court by calling out "jailbreak" when it throws the ball over to the opposite team. If the opposing team drops the ball, the throwing team's prisoner will be released from jail and allowed to come back onto the court. If the ball is caught, the prisoner will remain out of the game and the receiving team will take its turn. The game ends when a team has no players left on the court.

SAFETY PRECAUTIONS

Do not place more than 10 players on one side. Have the jail line form next to the center line.

Partners Up

This is a simple activity in which pairs of children work together to try to stand from various sitting positions.

EQUIPMENT
• none needed

GETTING STARTED:

Divide the class into pairs of children of similar size. Have the partners spread out around the room.

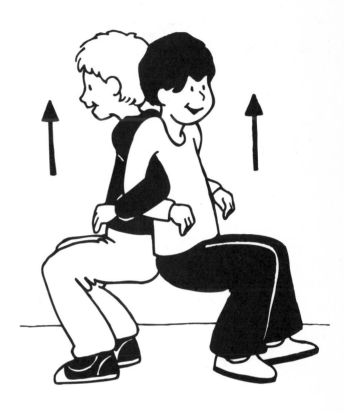

PROCEDURE:

Instruct each pair of students to sit on the floor back to back. Have the students link their elbows behind their backs. Tell them that their challenge is to stand up without letting go of one another's arms. They may think that this is easy—until they try it a few times. Explain that it takes cooperation and coordination.

As a variation, instruct the partners to sit face to face. They should place their legs in front of them so that their feet are touching their partners' feet. Be sure students bend their knees. Next, instruct them to hold hands. Now they are ready to try to stand up. Once they have become proficient at this, they are ready to combine pairs and try these tasks with four people.

SAFETY PRECAUTIONS
Try to match up students of equal height and size.

FS-32602 Indoor Play © Frank Schaffer Publications

Pass and Go

Students standing in groups of five to eight take turns passing the ball and running to the end of the opposite line.

EQUIPMENT
- one ball per game

GETTING STARTED:

For each game, assemble equal groups of five to eight players. Have the groups form lines and face each other.

PROCEDURE:

Hand the ball to the first student in one of the groups, who will throw it using two hands to the first student in the opposite line. After throwing the ball, the student must run to the end of the opposite line. This pattern continues until all of the students have returned to their original starting positions.

For subsequent rounds, vary the way the students pass the ball. Instruct them to bounce the ball, throw it with one hand, hit it with a fist, roll it on the ground, or kick it on the ground.

SAFETY PRECAUTIONS

Have all of the students run to their right when running to the end of the line in order to avoid collisions.

Rock, Paper, Scissors

This variation of tag incorporates the familiar Rock, Paper, Scissors game to determine which team chases the other.

EQUIPMENT
- cones or tape to mark the boundary lines

GETTING STARTED:

Divide the class into two teams. Line up the teams on opposite sides of the room behind their boundary lines. Familiarize your class with the traditional hand signals game of Rock, Paper, Scissors in which scissors cuts paper; paper covers rock; and rock dulls scissors.

PROCEDURE:

The players on each team will take turns selecting a hand signal—rock (closed fist), paper (hand stretched out flat), or scissors (two fingers spread apart). Once the signal chooser has made a decision, he or she will quietly tell it to his or her teammates. The two teams will then come to the center of the room, and on the count of three, the teams will display their signals. The team with the dominating signal will chase and try to tag the players on the other team. For example, scissors chases paper; paper chases rock; and rock chases scissors. If the teams choose the same signals, the match is a draw and play begins again with new signal choosers. When the signals are displayed, the students must determine whether they will chase or be chased. A team being chased must run to its side of the room. If a player being chased is tagged before reaching the line, he or she must go to the other team. Once all of the players have reached the line, start the game again with new signal choosers.

SAFETY PRECAUTIONS
Be sure the area is cleared of obstacles.

85

FS-32602 Indoor Play © Frank Schaffer Publications

Sew It Up

With the class standing in a large circle, one student acts like a "needle" to unite the students he or she passes between.

EQUIPMENT
- none needed

GETTING STARTED:

Have the students stand in a circle with their arms at their sides.

PROCEDURE:

Designate one student to stand outside of the circle. This student will be the "needle" who will run in and out of the circle. Each time the needle runs through the circle, the two players who are passed by the needle will join hands. The needle may not touch anyone in the circle or run through players who have already been sewn together. The needle continues to run in and out until the entire circle has been "sewn up." Start over and repeat until everyone has had the chance to be the needle.

86

Snakes

Working as pairs, as larger groups, and eventually as a whole class, the students link themselves together to form "snakes."

EQUIPMENT
• none needed

GETTING STARTED:

Divide the class into pairs. Explain to the students that they will pretend to be sections of a snake.

PROCEDURE:

Instruct each pair of students to lie on their stomachs in a line with their arms and legs stretched straight out. One member of each pair will hold on to the ankles of his or her partner. Each pair will practice moving together around the floor. Next, have each pair connect with another pair. Allow the four-person snakes to practice moving together. Then have each group connect with another group to form an eight-person snake. Finally, have the students connect all of the groups to create one large snake. Give the large snake several tasks to perform such as rolling onto its back without coming apart and curling up and going to sleep. The students must hold on to their partners' ankles while moving.

SAFETY PRECAUTIONS

Be sure that the floor is clear of any obstacles. If any students are having a difficult time moving around, place them at the front of the snake so that they can use their hands to help them move.

Spinning Disks

Students sitting in a circle of six to eight take turns spinning a plastic disk on the ground and calling on another group member to grab the disk before it stops spinning.

EQUIPMENT
- one plastic disk (or Frisbee) per group

GETTING STARTED:

Divide the class into groups of six to eight students. Arrange the groups so that they are sitting in circles around the room. Have each group count off around the circle so that each student has an individual number. Give each group a plastic disk, and have the students place it in the center of the circle.

PROCEDURE:

Instruct the number one player in each group to stand up and spin the disk. As soon as the disk is spinning freely, the spinner will call out the number of a group member and then sit down. That student will jump up, grab the disk before it stops spinning, spin the disk again, and call out another number. Have the students continue in this fashion until everyone has had at least one turn. Players must remain seated until their numbers are called. Group members should work cooperatively to keep the disk from falling over. Challenge the groups to keep the disk spinning for a given amount of time.

Straddle Ball

Students in groups of 10 to 15 take turns trying to roll a ball past the legs of another player, who attempts to block the ball with his or her hands.

EQUIPMENT
- two medium-sized foam balls per group

GETTING STARTED:

Divide the class into groups of 10 to 15 students. Arrange the students into circles so that the members of each group are facing one another. Have the students sit with their legs apart so that their feet are touching the feet of the people next to them. They will begin the game with their hands on their knees.

RULES:

Explain to the students that the object of the game is to roll the ball between the legs of another player before that player can stop the ball with his or her hands. Begin the game by giving the ball to a random student, who will roll the ball. The students must try to catch the ball and roll it through the legs of another player. The students may not hit or throw the ball in any way. They must keep their hands on their knees until a ball is rolled at them.

As a variation, place one student in the center of the circle with a ball. This person will try to roll the ball through the legs of any child. If a student allows the ball to go through his or her legs, he or she will trade places with the center person, and the game will continue.

Tag Games

These tag games are played with the entire class performing various movement skills while trying to tag one another or avoid being tagged.

EQUIPMENT
• none needed

GETTING STARTED:

There are many variations of tag that can be played indoors. Each game begins in the same fashion. The class is divided in half, and each half starts at opposite ends of the room. One student, who will be called "It," will be the tagger and will start the game in the middle of the room. Each game ends when there is only one person left who has not been tagged.

PROCEDURE:

When you give the signal, all of the students must run to the opposite ends of the room without being tagged by the person who is "It." Anyone who is tagged must join "It" in the center of the room and will become a tagger. When everyone has either reached his or her destination or been tagged, the new group of "Its" will assemble in the center of the room and play will resume.

SAFETY PRECAUTIONS

Be sure that the play area is large enough to accommodate the entire class and that it is free of obstacles.

To add to the fun, have your students try some of the following variations of basic tag:

Popcorn Tag: All students will move across the play area by hopping up and down on both feet. When a person is tagged, he or she will hold hands with the player who is "It" and form a chain. Together they will hop and try to tag other players.

Dog Tag: All students will move across the play area on their hands and knees. Tagged players will become "It."

Snake Tag: All students will move across the play area on their stomachs.

What Time Is It?

This activity helps younger students learn to tell time by using their bodies to create a human clock. Students also practice their cooperation skills with this activity.

EQUIPMENT
- one large clock or drawings of different times on clocks, paper, tape

GETTING STARTED:

Write the numbers 3, 6, 9, and 12 on separate sheets of paper. Create a large clock on the floor by taping the numbered sheets in the appropriate positions around the clock. Arrange the entire class in a circle around these numbers. Tell the students that they will be pretending to be a clock and that some students will be the hands while others will be the numbers. Explain the clockwise movement of a clock.

PROCEDURE:

Instruct the students to notice the number that is closest to where they are standing. Then have them move together in a clockwise direction. They should complete one full rotation so that, when they stop, they will be in their original positions.

Next, have the students work together to show times on the clock. Choose seven students to be the hands of the clock. Three students will make the hour hand and four will make the minute hand. Designate a small number of students to stand at the 12, another small group to be at the 3, and so on. Each group should stand in back of its number to help the students see the time. Instruct the "hands" to stand on the clock. Have the hands start at 12. Give them different, simple times on the hour and half hour, and help them to move and stand in the correct positions. If you have a clock, move the hands of the clock to match the time students are recreating.

When the first group of hands has successfully shown two or three different times, choose seven more students to be the hands of the clock. Repeat the activity. To increase difficulty, ask the clock hands to show more complicated times, such as 11:27.

SAFETY PRECAUTIONS
Have each group of hands work cooperatively when passing each other.

Who Is "It"?

This simple version of reverse tag helps students develop quick reflexes.

EQUIPMENT
- one small object such as a marble or an eraser

GETTING STARTED:

Have all of the students line up at one end of the room so that they are standing side by side, facing forward, with their hands held out in back of them.

PROCEDURE:

Quietly walk behind the lined-up students. Making sure all the students are facing forward, drop the object into the hand of a student. The student with the object will run to the opposite wall. As soon as the other students see who is "It," they should try to tag that player before he or she reaches the opposite wall. Continue playing until this player is tagged. Once tagged, "It" will start the next round by dropping the object into a peer's hand. He or she may not chase the new "It."

SAFETY PRECAUTIONS

Be sure the play area is free of obstacles.

Zig-zag Ball Toss

This is a ball-tossing activity that involves intermixing two teams so that team members are throwing balls to teammates in a zig-zag pattern.

EQUIPMENT
• two medium-sized balls

GETTING STARTED:

Divide the class into two teams, and line up the teams so that they are facing each other, about three feet apart. Next, mix the members of each team together so that each person is facing a member of the opposite team and has a member of the opposite team on either side. Give a ball to the first person in each line.

PROCEDURE:

Each team will pass the ball to its members in a zig-zag pattern down the lines. The teams will be passing the balls at the same time. Start by having the teams send the balls down the lines and back one time. For each subsequent round, have the teams complete this task an additional time. The first team to complete the task the given number of times per round will win the round.

SAFETY PRECAUTIONS

Instruct the students to toss the ball below their teammates' shoulders.

Jumping Waves

Working in groups of four to six, the students practice their eye-foot coordination and agility as they try to jump over moving jump ropes.

EQUIPMENT
• two jump ropes per group

GETTING STARTED:

Have the students place their jump ropes on the floor. One student will hold one end of both jump ropes, and a second student will hold the other end of the jump ropes. The remaining students will start as the jumpers.

PROCEDURE:

The rope holders will move the ropes on the floor to create waves. The jumpers must jump over the waves without touching the rope. When a jumper touches a rope, he or she will trade places with one of the rope holders.

To increase the challenge of the activity, have two or three groups combine to create four to six rows of waves. The jumpers must run through the entire set of waves one at a time. To make the task even more challenging, have the rope turners stand up and turn the ropes while the jumpers run through the waves. Every turner must have the opportunity to be a jumper, and every jumper must have a try at being a turner.

SAFETY PRECAUTIONS

Be sure there is sufficient space between the groups so that the students can jump safely over their ropes.

Balloon Soccer

This modified version of soccer uses balloons instead of balls and can be played by two teams of up to 15 players each.

EQUIPMENT
• two dozen balloons

GETTING STARTED:

Inflate all of the balloons before the beginning of the lesson. Arrange the two teams so that they are sitting in alternating rows of five players each across the floor. Designate one person from each team to play the goalie position. Have the goalies sit in opposite corners of the room.

RULES:

The object of this game is for the students to hit the balloon to their own goalie, who catches the balloon and must try to pop it by sitting on it. Each goalie who pops a balloon scores a point for his or her team. The game can be played without keeping score. The students must remain seated and may only use their hands to bat the balloon. Each time a balloon has been popped, designate a new person to be the goalie. Allow the students to keep playing until all of the balloons have been popped or the class time has expired.

SAFETY PRECAUTIONS

Keep the players at a safe distance from the goalie.

Cooperative Jump Rope

Level of difficulty: **moderate**

This version of jump rope involves groups of four to six students taking turns at jumping with a long rope in a continuous pattern.

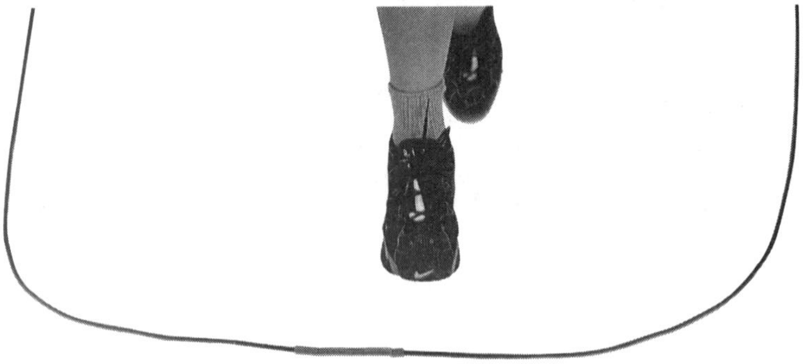

EQUIPMENT
- one long jump rope per group

GETTING STARTED:

Give each group a rope. Designate two students to start as the turners, and instruct the others to form a line away from the rope.

PROCEDURE:

The turners will begin turning the rope while the first person in line will take a turn at jumping. After about a minute, direct the jumper to trade places with a rope turner without stopping the rope. The next person in line will take a turn at jumping, and the original rope turner will go to the end of the line. Continue until everyone has had a chance at being both a rope turner and a jumper.

SAFETY PRECAUTIONS

Be sure the waiting lines are not too close to the turning rope.

FS-32602 Indoor Play © Frank Schaffer Publications

Crab Soccer

This easy-to-play game requires only minimal equipment and can be played either indoors or outdoors on a large square playing area. It is an ideal activity for the entire class to play together, in four squads of seven or eight players.

EQUIPMENT
- one large rubber ball, pencil, paper, stopwatch, four cones (optional)

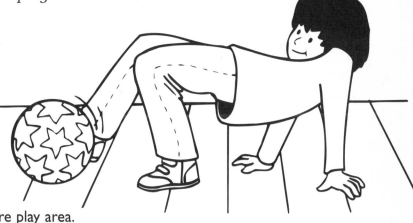

GETTING STARTED:

Use rope or cones to mark off a large square play area. Organize the students into four teams, and have them remove their shoes and sit around the edges of the square. Next, give a number to each student by counting off the members of each team. Each student should have a correspondingly numbered classmate on each of the other three teams. If one or more teams is short a player, give one of the players on the team a second number. Remind the students that it is very important for them to remember their numbers.

SAFETY PRECAUTIONS

Warn the students that they may not kick the ball above their heads. Never allow more than four players into the middle of the play area at any time.

RULES:

Only one player from each team may be in the playing area at a time. Call out a number to determine the offensive players for each round. These players must crab-walk (walk with their hands on the floor behind them and their feet out in front of them) to the center of the playing area, where they will attack the ball. Using only their feet, the players will try to knock the ball across the other teams' goal lines, which are defended by the remaining players sitting at the edges of the square. Defenders may use any part of their bodies, except for their hands, to deflect the ball. Offensive players may only touch the ball with their feet and may only move around the playing area by crab-walking. After each score, these players return to their goal lines and a new number is called. If the ball passes over a corner of the square, the ball must be replayed from the middle of the playing area. Any player who violates the rules must sit out for two minutes.

Footbag

This is a challenging foot game in which two to five players pass a small footbag (also known as a Hacky Sack) back and forth using only their feet. This is an excellent activity for developing eye-foot coordination, flexibility, and balance in older students.

EQUIPMENT
- one footbag per group (small beanbags will work)

GETTING STARTED:

Organize the students into groups of up to five players.
Distribute one footbag to each group.

PROCEDURE:

Show the students the two basic skills needed for this activity. The first skill is the inside kick, which is performed by dropping the bag straight down and kicking it up into the air with the inside of the foot. The second skill is the outside kick, which is performed by dropping the bag out to the side of the body and kicking it up into the air with the outside of the foot. For both kicks, the knee should be slightly bent, and the student should try to kick the bag close to the body. Instruct the students to take turns practicing each kick five times. Then have the students try to pass the bag back and forth to their partners using each kick. The only time the students may touch the bag with their hands is when they are putting it into play.

Challenge the students to see how many consecutive times they can kick the bag up into the air without the bag hitting the floor. Next, challenge the groups to see how many consecutive times they can pass the bag back and forth using each kick.

SAFETY PRECAUTIONS

Make sure there is sufficient space between students so that they cannot accidentally kick one another. Students should never kick above knee level.

Movement Mixer

This activity involves practicing individual movements, as well as cooperation and listening skills. Students will perform individual activities while part of a specified group.

EQUIPMENT
- stopwatch, megaphone (if available)

GETTING STARTED:

Have the students scatter around the room.

PROCEDURE:

Explain that when you call out a number, the students will quickly form into groups. They will know how many people to have in each group by listening to the number called. If they hear the number 4, they will need to form groups of 4 students each. Extra students can either stand to the side or join a group. Once in groups, explain that they will perform a specific movement for a set amount of time. They can do jumping jacks, knee bends, windmills (touching each hand to the opposite foot), hopping, and running in place. Illustrate each movement to be sure students know what to do.

Signal to students that the game is about to begin. Give them a movement to perform, and then call out a number. After the groups are formed and the exercise is accomplished, choose another skill for the students to perform and call out another number. Make sure that students form new groups each time a number is called and that they form the correct size groups.

SAFETY PRECAUTIONS
Remind students to spread out to avoid collisions.

Pass and Go Times Four

In this more complicated extension of Pass and Go, the students form four lines, take turns passing a ball to the first student in one of the other lines, and then run to the back of that line.

EQUIPMENT
• one ball per game

GETTING STARTED:

Divide the class into four groups, and have each group line up perpendicular to a different wall, with each student facing the center of the room. Leave an open area in front of the four lines, and designate one student to start the game in the center. Hand the ball to the center student.

RULES:

The student in the center will pass the ball to the first person in one of the lines and will then run to the end of that line. The student with the ball will run to the center, stop, and pass the ball to the first student in another line. This pattern of passing the ball to a different line and running to the end of that line will continue until everyone has been to the center.

SAFETY PRECAUTIONS

Have all students run to the right when running to the end of the line in order to avoid collisions.

FS-32602 Indoor Play © Frank Schaffer Publications

Relays

Relay activities involve groups of varying sizes participating cooperatively. These activities place a strong emphasis on students learning to perform well as individuals in order to contribute positively to the team. Each team member performs an individual task; however, a relay is completed only when all members have completed the assigned task.

The importance of group participation in relays makes them an excellent tool for promoting cooperation and camaraderie among students. Relays work only when participants strive together to achieve a common goal. Students can be very supportive of one another in this team atmosphere, often challenging each other to perform to the best of their abilities. By cheering their comrades to the finish line, students learn the great extent to which good will and cooperation can motivate a peer.

It is not necessary to single out a team for finishing a task first. It is more important to praise the success of students working together.

FS-32602 Indoor Play © Frank Schaffer Publications

Dog Race

In this activity, students, in teams of five, will complete a relay race while running on their hands and knees.

EQUIPMENT
• chalk or tape

GETTING STARTED:

Divide the class into teams of five players each. Using chalk or tape, designate a starting and finishing line. Line up the teams side by side at one end of the gym. Explain to the students that they will be running a dog race.

PROCEDURE:

The first student in each team will run to the opposite end of the gym on his or her hands and knees and back to the starting line. When a student returns to the starting line, he or she must tag the second student in line and then go to the end of the line. The second student runs the dog race course, and then tags the third student. The relay continues until the students have returned to their starting positions. Students must remain on their hands and knees throughout the relay.

SAFETY PRECAUTIONS
Remind the students to keep their heads up as they run so that they can see where they are going.

Hula-Hoop Challenge

Each group of five to seven students must pass a Hula-Hoop to all of its members while holding hands.

EQUIPMENT
- one Hula-Hoop per group

GETTING STARTED:

Divide the class into teams of five to seven players. Line up the teams side by side and hand the first person in each group a hoop. Instruct the students to hold hands.

PROCEDURE:

Explain to the students that the object of the relay is for each team to pass the hoop down the line without the team members breaking their hands apart. The hoop will be passed along the line like a bead on a string as students squat down and pick up their feet to let the hoop pass over and under them to the next person. When the last student in line has received the hoop, he or she will take it to the front of the line and will start the process again. The relay is over when the students have returned to their original positions.

SAFETY PRECAUTIONS

Be sure that the hoops are not damaged in any way. Check for cracks or jagged edges.

Hula-Hoop Mania

This is a relay race in which each group of four or five students will travel to a given point and back with a Hula-Hoop around their waists.

EQUIPMENT
- one Hula-Hoop per group, tape

GETTING STARTED:

Divide the class into groups of four or five students. With chalk or tape, designate a starting line. Line up the groups side by side at one end of the room. Give one hoop to the first person in each group. The race begins with one student in each hoop and continues until the entire group is inside.

PROCEDURE:

Explain to the students that the object of the relay is to move the hoop to the other end of the room and back to the starting line. The first player in each group will get inside of the hoop and carry it at waist level through the course. When that player returns, the second player in line will get inside the hoop with the first player, and so on, until everyone is inside the hoop and has completed the course.

For third and fourth graders, if there is not enough room inside the hoop, the players will hold on to the outside of the hoop as the group travels. To extend the relay for all, when all of the players are inside the hoop, continue the relay in reverse so that each time it reaches the starting line, a player gets out of the hoop and goes back in line. The relay continues until everyone is back in line.

SAFETY PRECAUTIONS

As more students amass inside the hoops, remind the students to slow down as they travel across the course.

104

Kangaroo Relay

Players work in teams to relay a ball into a basket by hopping with the ball between their knees.

EQUIPMENT
- one small to medium-sized ball per group, one trash can or box per group

GETTING STARTED:

Divide the class into two teams. Have the students line up at one end of the room. Place a wastebasket or box in front of each group. Give the first player in each group a ball.

PROCEDURE:

The first student in each team will place the ball between his or her knees and walk with the ball to the opposite end of the room and back again. The students may not touch the ball with their hands while they are moving. When the students return to the starting line, they must place the ball into the box without using their hands. The second student in line will pick up the ball and continue the relay, as the first student goes to the end of the line. The relay continues until the players are back to their original positions.

SAFETY PRECAUTIONS

Do not allow the students to run with the ball.

Logroll Relay

Students complete this relay in teams of five or six players while rolling like a log across the gym.

EQUIPMENT
• **none needed**

GETTING STARTED:

Line up the groups side by side at one end of the gym.

PROCEDURE:

Instruct the first student in each group to lie down on the floor so that his or her body is parallel to the opposite wall. Explain to the students that they will have to roll like logs across the floor. Remind them to take their time and try to roll straight so that they don't stray into other people. Each student must roll all the way across the floor and touch the opposite wall before rolling back to the starting line. When a student returns to the starting line, he or she will tag the next student, who will continue the relay. The relay ends when the students have returned to their original positions.

SAFETY PRECAUTIONS

To avoid collisions, make sure there is ample space between teams.

Madcap Relay

In this relay, students in groups of five or six must balance up to six plastic disks (or Frisbees) on their heads.

EQUIPMENT
- one plastic disk per student

GETTING STARTED:

Divide the class into groups of five or six students. Line up the groups side by side at one end of the room. Place one plastic disk per student at the opposite end of the room in piles directly in front of each group.

PROCEDURE:

In this relay, each student in turn must run to the opposite end of the room, place a disk on his or her head, and walk back to the group while balancing the disk on his or her head. (Allow the younger students to use their hands if needed.) When each student has brought a disk back to the group, the group members will place all of the disks in a stack at the front of the line. The next part of the relay requires that each student place all of the disks on his or her head while running to the opposite end of the room and back again. The students may use their hands to keep the disks on their heads. The relay continues until all of the students have completed this task.

SAFETY PRECAUTIONS
Be sure that there is sufficient space between groups.

FS-32602 Indoor Play © Frank Schaffer Publications

Penguin Relay

In this relay, each student in the group of four to six must carry a ball using only his or her feet.

EQUIPMENT
• one ball per group

GETTING STARTED:

Divide the class into groups of four to six students. Line up the groups so that they are standing side by side at one end of the room. Give the first student in each group a ball.

PROCEDURE:

Explain to the students that they must carry the ball using only their feet. The only time the students may touch the ball with their hands is when they are positioning it between their feet. Model this task for them, and point out to them how this will make them look like penguins because they will need to waddle back and forth. When given the signal to begin, the first student in each group will move the ball to the opposite wall and then back to the starting line, where he or she will place the ball at the feet of the next student in line. The first student will then go to the end of the line. The relay continues until everyone has returned to his or her original position. In subsequent rounds, have the students penguin-walk the ball either backwards or sideways.

SAFETY PRECAUTIONS

Be sure there is ample space between the groups for unobstructed waddlings.

Tunnel Crawl Relay

Each group of students creates a human tunnel through which each member of the team must crawl.

EQUIPMENT
- **none needed**

GETTING STARTED:

Divide the class into two large teams. Line up the two teams side by side toward the back of the room so that they are facing you.

PROCEDURE:

Instruct the students to stand an arm's distance from the teammate in front of them and to spread their legs slightly beyond their bodies so that they are creating a tunnel. When given the signal to begin, the last student in each line will crawl all of the way through the tunnel to the front of the line and stand up. The other players may not purposely touch the crawler. When the crawler has reached the front of the line, the group will call out "go," and the last student in line will crawl through the tunnel. The relay will continue until the players have returned to their original positions.

SAFETY PRECAUTIONS

If there are any students who are extremely small or extremely tall or large, it may be necessary for them to be placed on a specific team with students who are closer to their own size.

Ball Relays

Ball relays involve groups of five to eight students participating in cooperative ball-handling activities.

EQUIPMENT
• one small or medium-sized ball per group

GETTING STARTED:

Separate students into groups of five to eight students. Line up the groups side by side, and hand a ball to the first student in each group. Make sure students are evenly spaced apart at about an arm's length.

PROCEDURE:

For the first relay, explain to the students that each player will use both hands to pass the ball over the head to the next player in line. Explain that the players must pass the ball in the given manner. If the ball is dropped or passed in the wrong manner, it will be returned to the front of the line and the pattern must start over again. The ball will continue in this manner until it reaches the last player. This player will take the ball and run to the front of the line to start the process over again. This will continue until the players are back in their original positions.

The next relay involves passing the ball from side to side. The first player in line will pass the ball to the next person by holding it with two hands and turning to his or her right to make the pass. The second player in line will turn to his or her left to make the pass. This right and left pattern will continue until the ball reaches the last player in line. This player will run to the front of the line and start the pattern over again. This will continue until the players are back in their original positions.

FS-32602 Indoor Play © Frank Schaffer Publications

Another ball-relay variation is to have the students stand with legs apart to create a lane down the group line. The first player will roll the ball between his or her legs to the second player. Each player will continue to roll the ball until it reaches the last player in line. This player will run to the front of the line and start the pattern over again. This will continue until the players are back in their original positions.

Finally, get creative with the relays by combining the different tasks already performed to create different types of patterns. Create patterns that challenge the students to concentrate and use strong teamwork. For example, the ball will be passed over the head of the first student, to the right of the second student, rolled through the legs of the third and fourth students, and to the left by the fifth student to sixth student, and so on.

SAFETY PRECAUTIONS

Be sure there is sufficient distance between groups so that players will not run into one another. Be sure the area is clear of obstacles.

Newspaper Relay

This relay involves groups of students using newspaper squares as stepping stones.

EQUIPMENT
• newspapers

GETTING STARTED:

Before getting started, fold the newspapers into squares. Divide the class into groups of five or six students. Give the first student in each group two newspaper squares.

PROCEDURE:

In order to complete the relay, the students must use the newspapers as stepping stones. They will begin by standing on one newspaper square at the starting line in front of their teams. When they are given the start signal, the students will place the second square out in front of them. They must step to the second square and then reach back, pick up the first piece, and then place it out in front of them again. They will continue this process until they have reached the opposite end of the room, where they will turn around and continue back in the same manner to the starting line. Each student must then tag the next player in line, who will continue the relay. The relay will end when the students have all returned to their original positions.

SAFETY PRECAUTIONS

Be sure that the students place the newspapers within a reasonable distance so that they do not fall while attempting to reach the paper.

Parachute Activities

A parachute is a wonderful piece of equipment that will enhance any physical education program. Parachutes can be purchased at some teacher supply stores or ordered through catalogs. Parachutes can also be purchased at Army surplus stores.

Parachute activities help to increase flexibility, build endurance, and increase arm and shoulder strength. Most importantly, these activities are fun for children of any age.

Parachute Games

Level of difficulty: **simple**

The parachute activities described on the following pages will add an exciting and fun element to your physical education program.

EQUIPMENT
- one or more parachutes
- additional equipment needed is listed with each activity

GETTING STARTED:

Lay the parachute out on the floor, and have the students spread out evenly around its perimeter. Have the students grip the edge of the parachute with both hands and lift it to waist level. Count to three, and have the students lift the parachute over their heads and back down again. Allow the students to practice this several times. Then have the students practice shaking the parachute to create both large and small waves. Finally, have the students practice holding the parachute with one hand and walking around in a circle. Students can also practice skipping, hopping, and running around the circle while holding the parachute.

PROCEDURES:

Select five or six of the following activities for one class session. Each activity should last approximately five minutes. If time allows, encourage the students to repeat their favorite activities.

Popcorn

Have the students lay the parachute on the floor and sit around it. Place 15 to 20 small balls such as tennis balls, whiffle balls, and handballs on the parachute. Have each student grasp the edge of the parachute with both hands, stand up, and hold it at waist level. Then direct the students to shake the parachute until all of the balls bounce off it. Use the stopwatch to time how long it takes the students to complete this task. Challenge them to improve their time in subsequent rounds.

ADDITIONAL EQUIPMENT:
15–20 small balls, stopwatch

Ball Roll

Have the students stand in a circle around the parachute, holding it at waist level. Place a medium-sized ball on the parachute. Challenge the students to roll the ball in a circle around the edge of the parachute without allowing it to fall on the floor. After the ball has completed several circles, direct the students to change its direction. Use the stopwatch to time how long the students can keep the ball rolling.

ADDITIONAL EQUIPMENT: one medium-sized ball, stopwatch

Create a Dome

During this activity, the students will make a dome shape with the parachute and sit inside of the dome. Begin by laying the parachute flat on the floor. Have the students stand in a circle around the parachute. Instruct the students to bend down and grip the edge of the parachute. Next, tell them to work in unison to raise the parachute as quickly as possible and as high over their heads as possible. As the parachute fills with air, urge the students to step forward, pulling the parachute behind their backs as they move forward, and then to sit on the inside edge of the parachute. When this activity is performed properly, the parachute should hold the air inside itself, creating a dome over the students' heads.

Riding the Waves

Have the students hold the parachute at waist level. Tell them to imagine that the parachute is a great ocean. Choose two students at a time to crawl under the ocean. After each student has had a chance to crawl under the parachute, repeat the activity, but allow the students to simulate ocean waves by shaking the parachute as the crawlers move beneath it.

Snake in the Grass

Instruct the students to lay the parachute flat on the floor. Choose one person to be the snake in the grass. The snake must lie flat on his or her stomach in the middle of the parachute. Have the remaining students spread out and stand on top of the parachute. (To help prevent injuries, have the students remove their shoes.) No one may step off the parachute. The snake must slither around on his or her stomach and try to tag the other students. When a student is tagged, he or she also becomes a snake. Play continues until all of the students have become snakes.

FS-32602 Indoor Play © Frank Schaffer Publications

Floating Cloud

Have the students form a circle and hold the parachute at waist level. Instruct the students to bend down in unison, and then lift the parachute high over their heads while holding it tightly. Give a signal, such as a whistle blow, and have all of the students let go of the parachute at the same time. As the parachute floats through the air, the students will move to the middle of the circle and sit down. When the parachute lands, it will cover the students like a blanket.

Changing Colors

Instruct the students to spread out around the parachute so that each student is holding on to a different color from that of his or her neighbor. Have the students raise the parachute over their heads. Then call out one of the parachute's colors. When the students hear the color they are holding, they must release the

ADDITIONAL EQUIPMENT: The parachute must be multicolored.

parachute and run underneath the parachute to another section of the same color. For example, if the color blue is called, all of the students holding a blue section will release the parachute, run to another blue section, and grip the edge of the parachute at the new section. Repeat this activity until every color is called at least twice.

Cat and Mouse

For safety reasons, this activity should be played on a matted area and the students should remove their shoes. The activity will work best with younger children. Instruct the students to kneel on the mat while holding on to the parachute. Designate two or three students to be "mice" and one student to be the "cat." The mice will crawl around underneath the parachute, the cat will crawl on top of the parachute, and the remaining students will shake the parachute. The cat must try to tag all of the mice. When all of the mice have been tagged, pick different students as the cat and mice. Repeat until all of the students have had the chance to be either a cat or a mouse.

Merry-Go-Round

Instruct the students to hold the parachute with one hand at waist level and face in the same direction. Assign specific movements such as walking, running, hopping, skipping, and galloping, and have the students perform each movement while still holding the parachute with one hand. Change the task for each rotation of the parachute. For variety, have the students hold the parachute at different levels while completing the various movements.

116

Parachute Fitness Activities

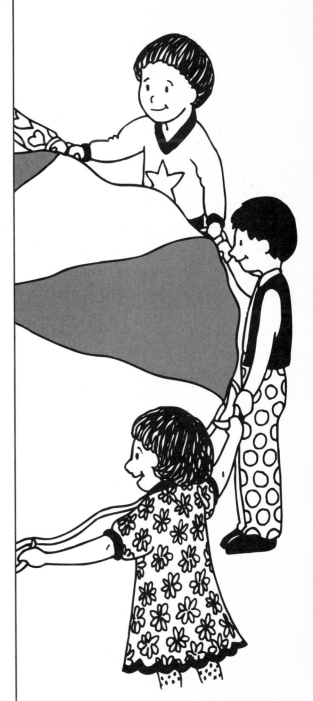

Parachute Pull

Instruct the students to stand with their feet about shoulders' width apart while holding the parachute at waist level. When you give the signal, the students will all pull the parachute toward themselves and hold this position for 10 seconds. Repeat this activity two or three times.

Reverse Pull

Have the students begin by holding the parachute at waist level. Instruct the students to turn and face away from the parachute while holding it over their heads. On the count of three, have them pull the parachute and hold this position for 10 seconds. Repeat two or three times.

Roll Up

Instruct the students to hold the parachute at waist level. When you give the signal, the students will roll up the parachute as quickly as possible by rolling the fabric hand over hand while working toward the center of the parachute. When everyone has reached the center, have the students completely unroll the parachute. Repeat two or three times.

Sit Ups

Have the students place the parachute flat on the ground. Instruct them to sit down with their legs underneath the parachute while holding on to the edge. Then have the students perform a specific number of abdominal crunch sit-ups. Repeat two or three times.

Toe Touchers

Have the students sit on the floor with their feet under the parachute. Next, direct them to pull the parachute up to their chins. Then have them bend forward, touch their hands (still holding the parachute) to their toes, hold this position for a count of 10, and return to the chin pull position.

FS-32602 Indoor Play © Frank Schaffer Publications

ACHIEVEMENT AWARDS AnD PROGRESS FORMS

Achievement Awards and Interest Forms

The use of achievement awards and progress forms are excellent opportunities for boosting a physical education program. Achievement awards should be given to individual students for individual success. When used appropriately and sparingly, these tools can provide a positive boost to any student's self-esteem. Interest forms should be used to track individual skill development and to explore personal interest in athletics.

Achievement Awards

Achievement awards should be given to students for such things as personal achievement, good sportsmanship, and positive attitude. Receiving an individual achievement award can help strengthen the confidence of any student. Children enjoy recognition and will be motivated to perform at a higher level when they know they have the opportunity to be singled out from their peers.

Try to present the award to no more than one or two students at a time. Spread the presentations out over a long period of time so that they do not lose their meaning. Make sure that every student has received at least one award over time. Present the certificate in front of the class and say a few words about why the student deserves the award.

Interest Forms

Interest forms are useful tools for encouraging students to take an active part in their fitness development. The forms will guide the students in creating goals for themselves and documenting their progress toward those goals.

A fitness contract can be a helpful tool to interest children in tracking their own physical progress. Using the fitness contract contained in this book or one of your own design, have each student sign a document stating his or her commitment to exercise and to healthy eating. Often, children will be eager to take "legal" responsibility for their own well-being. Ask them to bring the document home to be signed by a "witness," or a parent or guardian.

FS-32602 Indoor Play © Frank Schaffer Publications

Another useful way to help children think about physical education is to have them to consider the exercise they receive from their daily routine. You can further this line of thought by asking students to consider the specific movements involved in each exercise. For example, if a child plays tag after school, point out that he or she is exercising his or her leg muscles. Considering each exercise in separate movements helps facilitate a greater understanding of movement and exercise in general.

Finally, keep a record of physical activities for your class. You may want to keep track of different teams in your classroom, note the athletic development of individual students, keep track of awards given to different students, and so on.

Several examples of both achievement awards and interest forms can be found on the following pages. Please modify them to suit your needs.

My Fitness Contract

My name is _____ and I am _____ years old. By signing this contract, I show that I understand it is very important to take care of my own body. I agree to take responsibility for my own fitness. I will be sure to stretch out before and after I exercise to help prevent injury. I will build a strong heart and lungs with activities like jumping rope, bike riding, and walking or running with an older friend or parent. I will develop muscle strength by practicing pull-ups, push-ups, and sit-ups. If possible, I will also participate in games and sports that require movements like throwing, catching, or running to further develop my muscle strength.

I further agree to eat well in order to help my body grow. I will ask my parent or guardian to help me eat every day 2–4 servings of fruits; 3–5 servings of vegetables; 2–3 servings of protein such as meat, eggs, dry beans, and nuts; 2–3 servings of milk or cheese; and 6–11 servings of breads, cereal, rice, or pasta. I will try to remember to drink a lot of water, too.

I fully understand this form and willingly sign below, marking my agreement to these terms. By also signing below, my parent or guardian agrees to help me in this endeavor.

_____
Signature   Date

_____
Parent/Guardian Signature   Date

Official Document

Exercise Your Mind!

Keep a record of all the physical activity you do in one day, such as playing volleyball in P.E. class or playing on a soccer team after school. Remember that sometimes you exercise without even thinking about it, like when you play tag at recess or ride your bike to school. List each activity on the left side of the table. Mark an X in the correct column for each part of the body you exercised during each activity. Often you will mark more than one body part for just one activity. For example, if you ride a bike, you are exercising the muscles in your legs and feet.

Activity	Arms	Hands	Shoulders	Neck	Legs	Feet

During one day, how many times do you exercise your arms? _____ hands? _____

shoulders? _____ neck? _____ legs? _____ feet? _____

Which body part do you exercise the most? _____

Is there any area you think you need to exercise more? _____
any part less? _____

Physical Education Record Sheet

Name									

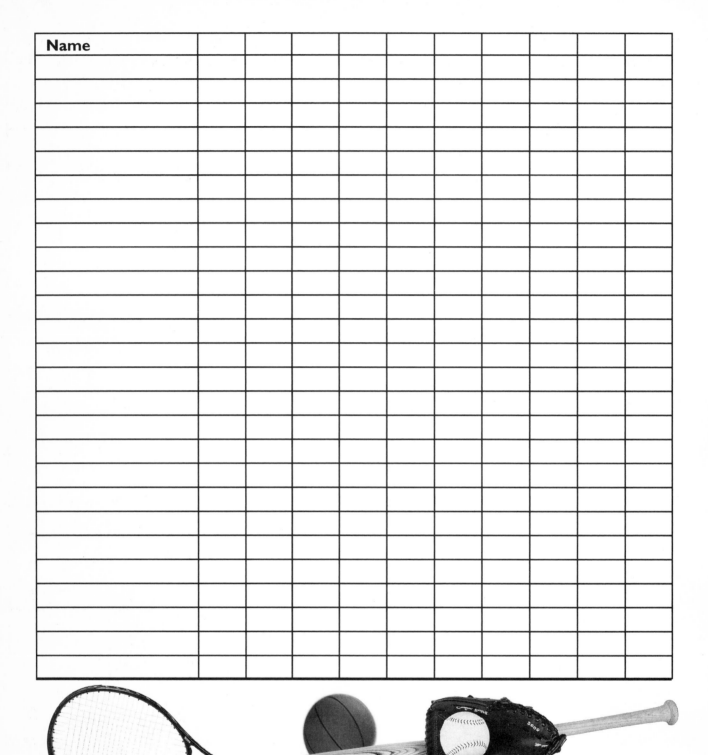

Teacher's Note: Use this form to help you organize your classroom physical activities. You can use it to keep track of individual students, of different classroom teams, and so on.

FS-32602 Indoor Play © Frank Schaffer Publications

FITNESS CHALLENGE FORM

Name _____

1.	Push-ups	Date	Full	Modified	Date	Full	Modified	Date	Full	Modified

2.	Abdominal Crunches	Date	Total	Date	Total	Date	Total

3.	Jump Rope	Date	Time	Date	Time	Date	Time

4.	Pull-ups	Date	Pull-up	Hang	Date	Pull-up	Hang	Date	Pull-up	Hang

5.	Long Jump	Date	Distance	Date	Distance	Date	Distance

FS-32602 Indoor Play © Frank Schaffer Publications

The Good Sportsmanship Award

awarded to

_____

on this date

_____

by

Award for Excellence in Sports

awarded to

_____

on this date

_____

by

_____

"I Did It" Award

awarded to

_____

on this date

_____

by

_____